THE LIFE OF A REFUGEE, IMMIGRANT AND WRITER

Christa Baier

Author's Tranquility Press
MARIETTA, GEORGIA

Copyright © 2022 by Christa Baier.

All rights reserved. No part of this publication may be reproduced, distributed or transmitted in any form or by any means, including photocopying, recording, or other electronic or mechanical methods, without the prior written permission of the publisher, except in the case of brief quotations embodied in critical reviews and certain other noncommercial uses permitted by copyright law. For permission requests, write to the publisher, addressed "Attention: Permissions Coordinator," at the address below.

Christa Baier/Author's Tranquility Press
2706 Station Club Drive SW
Marietta, GA 30060
www.authorstranquilitypress.com

Ordering Information:
Quantity sales. Special discounts are available on quantity purchases by corporations, associations, and others. For details, contact the "Special Sales Department" at the address above.

The Life of A Refugee, Immigrant And Writer/Christa Baier
Paperback: 978-1-959453-39-0
eBook: 978-1-959453-42-0

    The street was unusually quiet, considering it was early afternoon on a sunny September day. None of the usual noises from pedestrians or moving vehicles were audible, all windows were shut and not a single face peered behind drawn curtains. In the middle of the street was a traffic isle, almost completely covered by a big pile of beige sand. The only sign of life was a little girl, who discovered the latest spot for her to play. Being at home by herself without toys, except, for one doll she had received for her 5th birthday over a year ago from her godmother. Unfortunately, she was not allowed to play with that doll, because it was made of porcelain, with real hair, with all movable joints and it was as tall as she was, therefore impossible for her to handle by herself. For that reason, she found it naturally a good idea to leave the small apartment and look for things to do outside. After discovering the pile of sand from the living room window she went out to play, even though no other children were in sight. Unaware of her surroundings and completely engrossed in shoveling sand with a shiny soup spoon, she never noticed the far off sound of an approaching airplane, whose engine noise was growing louder and louder with each passing second. But then she was startled by a sudden rat-tat-tat sound and watched as small handfuls of sand were erupting to the left and right of her, that seemed like moved by magic. She wondered what caused the sand to spray up on its own, looked up and saw a plane pass over her head, just barely above the rooftops of the three and four story buildings. By then the roar of the engine was so loud, she instinctively covered her ears with her hands while watching the plane starting to turn around at the end of the street. Before she could form another thought, she felt herself being scooped up by strong hands and rushed off the street, as the plane had completed its turn and came flying low to possibly hit the intended target, which was obviously missed the first time. While cursing under his breath he carried her into the basement of the three-story building, which served as an air raid shelter. She soon realized it was Mr. Goldmann, the tall and usually friendly landlord of the building, where she and her mother shared a small apartment. She remembered last Christmas while being sick with a rash that covered her entire body, and mother applying a yellow colored salve all over her. There was a knock at the door and in came Saint Nikolas, wearing a long red coat trimmed with fur and a pointed hat. She was standing on a stool dressed in pajamas, when he asked if she had been a good girl all year, while shaking a switch at her to make sure she spoke the truth. As he turned his head to glance at mother, she saw there was a familiar face behind the Saint Nikolas mask, and without fear she greeted him with a "hi, Mr. Goldmann". Most of the other tenants were assembled in the basement, which was sparsely lit by a few candles they brought with them. She could hardly make out the faces of the people and the air smelled musty, like clothes that had been put away after a season ended and later brought out of hiding to air out. Hastily packed suitcases and various bundles, that most likely contained some prized possessions, were held close by their owners. Now the returning plane could be heard again as it made one more pass over the entire length of the street. The noise of the engine was growing weaker but kept on resounding in her ears.

The steady drone of engines was interrupted by the soft voice of a flight attendant, who asked if I wanted anything to drink, and to inform me that dinner would be served in approximately thirty minutes. I had been brought back to the present again, after day dreaming with my eyes wide open, except it was not a dream. Wow, I thought, as I smiled to myself, that little girl was really me. I had not mentally re-visited any part of my childhood in a long, long time, there were not all that many good times to remember. But more and many more memories were bound to spring into the forefront of my thoughts, because I was on my way to a reunion with my two brothers, Karl-Heinz, who is eighteen months younger than I, and Lothar, who is seven years younger than I am. Our lives took us in all different directions. We had not seen each other for a while and were planning to revisit some places of our childhood. However, a visit to my mother at this time was not in our discussed plans, but first on the agenda was a road trip to lower Bavaria, where we wound up after evacuating our home town in February of 1945, just three months before the end of World War II in Germany. We lived in that region until about February 1947. I do recall those approximately two years being the best part of my early childhood, even with all the hardship we suffered during those trying times. My youngest brother Lothar would not really remember anything about that part of our lives, because he was just about six months old at the time, we had to leave our small apartment in the city of Goerlitz. Right now, only about twenty-five minutes into an eight hour flight, I had the perfect opportunity to reflect on the many events of my childhood before my arrival in Frankfurt, Germany, then on to a connecting flight to Hamburg, the meeting and starting point of our adventure. But first and foremost, I was very anxious and full of anticipation about the reunion. Yet for some strange reason I could not mentally focus on the faces of my two brothers, instead I found myself once again in the air raid shelter and reminiscing about the past events of that afternoon so long ago.

After Mr. Goldmann rescued me, we sat in the air raid shelter for some time. I did hear some snippets of various conversations about dive bombers and whispers, purposely muffled, about the carelessness of some parents who would leave a six-year-old child unattended during times like these. Air raids were common place, but mostly happened during the night. The "all clear" siren sounded, and everyone returned to their apartment, lugging their stuff back into their own little world and glad another raid on the city was over without any bombs falling in the immediate neighborhood, and hopefully no casualties. Several days before the air raid, I had been busy on the huge steel bridge that was perpendicular to our street and our apartment building. This location gave us a very nice view of the river that flowed through the city. I had spotted several huge cylindrical objects many feet apart of each other.

They actually reached from one end of the bridge to the other and were connected by wires. Escaping the confines of our little apartment I pretended they were horses, like those at a circus, and hoisted myself onto one of them. In my imagination I galloped back and forth across the bridge, I was a bare back rider in a circus, standing tall with my arms stretched out on both sides. Later I found out that my metal "horses" actually were bombs intended to blow up the bridge to prevent the approaching Russian army from entering the city.

Well, on the evening following the air raid and time in the shelter, mother got quite an earful about the events of the day from the landlord, and I received a sound spanking for having left the apartment. "You, miserable brat," she hissed, "from now on you will be locked in." Sure enough, I was locked in the living room with access only to the little bedroom where Karl-Heinz and I slept when he was not in foster care. A couple open-faced sandwiches on a plate, neatly cut into quarters, had to last all day while mother was at work. Unfortunately, there was no way to get to the toilet, instead I had to use a potty that was under my bed. I had never been a sloppy child, therefore, after having used that potty for the first occurrence of nature, I could not bring myself to use it again without it having been emptied first. I simply had to do something about that, but I was locked in. Looking around the room the only option was very clear to me. It needed to be emptied, so I opened the window wide and dumped the contents out of our third floor window. It seemed a good thing to do at the time, however, the window faced the front of the building and was in direct line with the entrance to a small grocery store at street level. This caused great distress to some passersby and, of course, to the landlord, who just had to inform Mother about my latest activity. I had no clue why I was getting another spanking until it was almost over, but between slaps she made it very clear to me. I had never seen mother in such a rage, but I always did have an uneasiness and great fear of her since my earliest recollections. It seems to have something to do with a real fear of water, and I felt my grandmother had saved my life at least on one occasion from drowning. This was just a childish fear, I thought to myself, because I don't think anyone has ever drowned while having her hair washed and rinsed in a basin full of water. What I do remember vividly is having my head held under water longer than usual. I was just about to run out of breath when all at once the grip loosened. My grandmother, whom I lovingly called Omi, had made a surprise visit. A great deal of shouting between the two women gave me a chance to retreat to the bedroom, with wet hair still uncombed. Just then another incident was suddenly on my mind, and I had the urge to tell my Omi about it. The voices from the other room were muffled by now, so I did not want to start more argument. The other "incident" had to do with being on the river with Mother in a row boat on a sunny afternoon, about a summer or so earlier. My mother was rowing, and I was really enjoying the ride, when she suddenly began to rock the boat from side to side. A wave of real concern came over me and I gripped the edge of the wooden seat really tight. I looked at her face and she smiled back at me but began to rock with more force. By now I was really scared and began to cry, while she started to laugh. The more I cried, the more she laughed and kept on rocking. I don't remember anything else of that day, but the fear of being near any water had stayed with me for many years. What I do remember is being envious of my brother Karl-Heinz, who is one and a half years younger than I and got to stay with a foster mother. She took in foster children due to various circumstances of their families. At that particular time, he was the only child living with her, and I loved visiting and playing with all the wonderful toys at her place on occasional weekends. There was a bright red fire truck in the huge, empty attic to ride in. I used to beg my brother to let me have a ride once around the attic. In the apartment was another great surprise, a life-sized pony rocking horse, which was covered in real horse hide. Oh, how I envied my brother for living with Mommy Deen, a somewhat short and stocky lady, who absolutely loved children. Her name was Frieda Krien, but that was a little hard to say for us, so we simply called her Mommy Deen, not exactly to mothers liking. Being locked in mother's apartment all day was lonely and I had only one doll, which I was not allowed to play with unsupervised.

The last time there was any fun and excitement was when mother suddenly got married. I did not know she was involved with anyone, after all, I was just a little kid. Mother's uncle Franz, a master tailor, made the wedding dress and the suit for the couple, even I got two dresses for the occasion. From what I heard, the groom was from Holland, over six feet tall and in the army. He was on leave when they got married, but the honeymoon was very short lived, and I don't think mother told him that she had two children. He had only seen me around the apartment, and as it turned out he did not like kids. To the best of my recollection, he did save me from a good spanking. While the adults celebrated the wedding day I played outside with other children and inadvertently ripped a small triangle in the back of my new dress while climbing a fence. When I was called in for the evening, I slinked up the stairs, being very careful that my back was to the wall, so mother would not see the rip in the dress at my backside. Well, that did not work, so before she could raise a hand, he suggested that instead of a spanking on their wedding day she should lock me in the rumpus room. An hour in there should be an enough punishment, he said. That suggestion made me immediately like him, and to my surprise she agreed with him. Things seemed to start looking up for me. Without further discussion I was locked in the tiny room, which contained unwanted pieces of furniture and other household items. But there was no light and no window, therefore it took a while before my eyes got used to the darkness. So, I just stood still in the center of the room for a while. I did wish for some matches, because I was quite adept at lighting them.

Our apartment was in a very old house that had no electricity on the upper most floor, and during the months when it got dark before mother came home from work, I lit the gaslight fixture. This was no easy task, but I had watched mother light the gas lamp many times. First, I had to climb from a chair onto the kitchen table, which was located directly under the light fixture. Next, I deftly lit a match and very carefully open the gas nozzle just a little bit. A hissing sound let me know the gas was on, but you could also smell it. Then, with a steady hand, I brought the lit match ever so gently to a white mesh "sock," all the while being careful not to touch it. If you did, the delicate material would disintegrate to powder and there would be no light. I knew this was a delicate maneuver and I suppose I could have blown the roof off the house, but mother never mentioned any of such danger. The room was illuminated, and that was important to me.

Back in the rumpus room it seemed as if hours passed in the dark, and I really thought they forgot about me. But finally, I was rescued and sent to bed without any dinner. No matter, I was not hungry at that time anyway. Before falling asleep I thought about thanking my new stepfather for coming to my rescue and hoped he would be around for a long time. As it turned out, a three-week courtship was not a good foundation for everlasting wedded bliss, and the honeymoon was turning sour. Daily arguments shattered hopes of a nice family life and the Dutchman became more demanding of mother. He wanted a foot bath prepared every evening and the water temperature was not always to his liking. One evening he wanted more hot water added to the basin, but mother did not like his commanding tone. She simply poured scalding hot water not only into the basin, but purposefully directly onto his feet. He let out a painful whimper, collected himself and the ensuing fight was something to remember. His dinner had to be ready at a certain time and to make matters worse, mother had told him that her son would be living with us from now on. Mommy Deen was leaving the city in these uncertain times, and since my brother was not her own, she returned him to us with tears in her eyes. Her eyes were not the only ones filled with tears. Well, now that Karl-Heinz was back to live with us, at least I had company during the day. The arguments between mother and her husband grew louder and more often. Then suddenly, he was called back to active duty, his leave was over and so was the marriage. She was named the guilty party in a granted divorce in abstention.

The separation from Mommy Deen was traumatic and full of tears for both, Karl-Heinz and me, because now I had no place to visit for the occasional weekend, filled with caring hugs, delicious food and playtime. It must have been twice as hard for my brother, who was not used to the harsh living environment with our mother. I do recall that after his first day of school, while walking home, he soiled his pants. Needless to say, Mother was not enthused about something that was repeated frequently until he grew out of that smelly habit. Mother, what can I say about her? Except that she was more complicated than most mothers were in those days. Even as a child, being the eldest of five, she displayed a strong-willed challenge for her parents. It was told she had a somewhat mean streak in her, which she displayed since early childhood with aggressive behavior towards her siblings. Coupled with an unattractive amount of selfishness to the extreme, that carried over into most of her adulthood, did not make her the most liked by her siblings, three sisters and one brother. Unfortunately, I do not remember ever having meet my father, except when I was just a toddler, he was killed during World War II, when I was still too young to remember him. I just know her as a strong person in body and mind, but a petite and attractive woman of medium height, with an elegant walk and enough sway in her hips to attract a second look of men who passed her in the street. Her fierce independence, I assume, was the single most reason for her distaste towards marriage, and the long-range expectance of having to be there for a partner in life. One thing was absolutely and painfully clear: she never ever wanted any children. Once, while in a seldom jovial mood, she confessed about having dreams of being a trapeze artist with a circus and traveling the world. That statement helped clarify the fact she had no interest or desire to be a housewife with all its duties, especially cleaning the house. Washing floors, dusting and washing dishes on a daily basis were definitely not chores she liked, and would put them off as long as possible. I really think she was hoping for me to grow older fast so I could do these things. But there is at least one thing in which she excelled, besides the love for dancing and having a good time. She had a very strong work ethic and I have never known for her not to have a job and maximum earning power through overtime work. It was questionable though how she saved or spent the fruits of her labor. She was good at finding nice material and had her Uncle Franz make her a dress or skirt fitting her perfectly. If there was a little left over, he would make sure I got a little skirt or a blouse out of it. Besides the absolutely most necessary expenditures, nothing extra was ever spent on her unwanted children. In later years, I got to admire her uncanny ability to sit and watch a movie in a darkened theater, while knitting a little undershirt for my youngest brother, without dropping a stitch. I admired that greatly. I hardly had any clothes to my name. I was full of expectation and excitement whenever a package arrived from America. Mother's youngest sister had met an American service man, who was stationed in Bavaria. They did get married after he sponsored her immigrating to the States about two years later. This resulted in a windfall for us and my grandmother in the form of arriving packages to us, containing very valued goodies, namely chocolate and chewing gum, not to mention articles of clothing that I wore proudly, and coffee for Omi.

By now, it is November of 1944 and last July we got an addition to our little family. I did not notice anything out of the ordinary, but suddenly I had a baby brother. It became my job to take care of the little guy while mother was at work, but mostly I kept him from crying by dipping his pacifier into the sugar bowl. At one time his entire face was sugar coated, he was a real sweet baby that time. Soon after the factory mother worked at was closed, the schools had done the same several months before and were being used as housing for soldiers stationed in the city or stood empty. One thing was absolutely certain for me: I did not miss going to school. Not that I minded going there, it was fun being with other children, but homework was an absolute torture time for me. Mother stood over me like a hawk while I was trying to figure out the correct answer for some addition and subtraction problems. Every time I wrote the wrong answer on my little slate tablet I got hit on the head or slapped in the face, always followed by verbal tirades about my stupidity. Finally, I thought I found the perfect solution to my problem. It was so simple. If I did not go to school, I would not have any homework, so there! The next day I left the apartment on time, but just a few houses down the street I ducked into a house and hid in the long hallway behind a couple bicycles. Quietly, I waited for hours in a most uncomfortable position, until I heard the kids return from school. I came out of hiding, joining them and walked home. That was the first and last time I played hooky, because I barely had my foot in the door when mother grabbed me and I got the beating of my life, again. How did she find out so fast? I did not dare ask, there was never a good time to disagree or question any of her decisions. The nightly air raids continued, and it got to be harder for me to leave my warm bed, get dressed while still half asleep, then take my already packed school bag and head for the basement. All this activity was well rehearsed, or so it seemed. This would occur anywhere from one to three times a night, just about every night, while every day loudspeakers mounted on the roofs of police cars were passing through the neighborhood to announce that residents must get ready to leave the city very soon. The reason given was because of news that the enemy was getting closer. One day mother's girlfriend Kate came to visit, but their conversation was interrupted by something going on in the street below. I could tell by the expression on their faces that something very disturbing was happening. They rushed to the window to see what was going on and I wanted to have a look as well. After squeezing between the two women and raising myself on tiptoes, I saw what appeared like a never-ending stream of people of all ages walking in the middle of the street and then cross the bridge. They were dressed shabbily, and some appeared to be wearing potato sack materials and tied with a piece of rope around the waist instead of a belt. A few oxen pulled some wagons with straw or hey, I could not tell which, and on top lay old people and some children. They did not look well, and even some who walked seemed to need the help of others to keep moving. There were also a couple goats and a cow with a red and swollen udder, she was mooing in a most painful way. Even more disturbing of all was the sight of men in uniforms, with shiny boots and carrying some kind of whips. Every few seconds one of them would swing a whip over the poor people's heads and onto their backs to make them move faster, not allowing even one to stop and milk the cow to relieve her pain. I could hardly believe my eyes that some of these men could be so cruel to other humans. Mother pushed me away from the window before I could ask any questions, and at the same moment she yelled: "you animals, you call yourselves soldiers!" Kate grabbed mothers' arm and pulled her back and away from the window. "Do you want to be walking with those poor souls," she said to her, "Think about your kids." I have never been able to get that picture of sheer misery and outright brutality out of my mind. Where were these people taken to and why? Even though I did not understand what was happening in the street below, it made me wonder how grown-ups could act in such brutal ways. How could I, being only six years old when this occurred. I could not sleep that night, instead I kept seeing that never ending mass of people being whipped to move faster. At some point I must have fallen into a restless sleep, the next noise I heard was the by now familiar sound of sirens, and Mother shaking me awake and urging me to dress in a hurry. It was my job to carry my school bag on my back, take my brother by the hand and head for the basement that was our air raid shelter. Mother followed with the baby and a suitcase filled with I don't know what. All this in total silence from the third floor, while the adults were listening for the sound of planes in the air raid shelter. On the second floor lived an older, and very heavy, lady. I never saw her go to the shelter. When school was still open, I would see her every morning standing at her open door as I was on my way out. Because she was so heavy and could not bend down, she would ask me to tie her shoes, which I did gladly and received a candy for doing so. I often wondered what would happen if a bomb actually fell on our house, would she be dead and were we safe just a few floors below. After all, clear siren sounded everyone went just as quietly back to their apartment and hopefully back to sleep.

On a miserably cold and still dark February morning, we had to leave our apartment. It was rumored that day was to be the very last chance to leave. There would not be another train to evacuate people. We walked a long way to the train station. My mother pushed the baby carriage, which was filled with some necessities and baby Lothar lay on top, covered with a feather pillow. Karl-Heinz and I held on to the carriage on either side, plus I carried my school bag on my back, which turned out to be stuffed to capacity with diapers for the baby. I had hoped to bring my one and only doll along, but she was rather tall and heavy. Besides, I knew she would be waiting for me when we returned. Pandemonium was the only way to describe the situation at the train station. The train was full and almost ready to pull out, when I suddenly realized I was separated from the rest of my family. Before panic set in I felt myself being lifted and handed through a window and finally reunited with my family. The next four days and nights the train just kept on moving, as conditions were worsening in every way possible. At times the train would back track, allowing a crew of emergency workers to replace sections of the track that had been bombed and ripped apart just hours before. Finally, we would move forward again until the next emergency repair. A stopped train became an easy target for the attacking low flying planes, who were almost constantly bombing cities and railways. At one point we slowly passed a train that had been the target by low flying aircraft and was ablaze from front to back. There were no apparent survivors.

The adults kept the children away from the windows. Every city and village we passed appeared to have just been bombed. The ruins of once intact buildings were still smoldering and looking ghostly without roofs, doors or windows. Once tall trees were now slightly taller than stumps and still burning or smoldering. All this was around the once beautiful city called Dresden, which had suffered one of the most brutal attacks by air. In one night over ten thousand civilians lost their lives when showered by incendiary bombing. Then we passed another train which stood in flames, with the locomotive knocked off its track. When we did stop once, people were getting off in droves to relieve themselves alongside the train or in a ditch. Because the toilets froze up with piles of feces on top of the ice in the unheated train, sanitary conditions became critical. Many suffered already from dysentery, my brother Karl-Heinz among them, but all were urged back onto the train sooner than they wanted. People ran out of food, children cried day and night. My brother said he slept just fine in the luggage net above our seats, but I was most uncomfortable on the hard wooden bench in the third-class section of that train. Mother made her way forward to the locomotive and got a tin cup full of water from the boiler. She was warned that the water may not be suitable for consumption, but she felt it was better than watching her baby die from dehydration and hunger. She and I took turns holding the cup over a lit candle to warm the water, then she poured a little farina into it and fed that mush to the baby. That was the only nourishment he got for days, but it kept him alive. A nice lady gave Karl-Heinz and me a walnut, which I was going to save for the next day, but it disappeared during the night. I spend considerable time searching for my lost treasure. I was sure someone must have stolen it from me while I slept, it was gone. This was not a train headed for a vacation destination, and except for crying small children there was hardly any conversation among the adults. In the daytime I spent hours looking out of the closed window and noticed that every time we crossed a river some bundles were thrown off the train and landed in the water. Most of them were wrapped in white pieces of bed linen material, others in whatever the people had with them. I asked mother what was in the bundles. She told me they were wrapped up babies who died from illness and hunger, and that was the way they had to be "buried." This really had me thinking. Why would anyone throw dead babies away, why not wait and bury them when we got off the train? I found the answers very soon. Dead bodies were not allowed to be kept on the train for fear of diseases, and inspectors constantly walked from one rail road car to the next and check. For lack of anything else to do I had started to count the bundles each day every time we crossed a river. With the help of an older girl, we summed it up to be around thirty-three bundles in four days, but we were sure we had missed a few that were thrown out the windows on the other side. When the train finally did stop and we were told to get off, we had no idea where we had landed. Hundreds of people were herded into long barrack type buildings and assigned to rows of bunk beds, which leaned precariously as if to meet in the middle. They were being kept upright by wedging a four-foot-long board between them. This was a refugee center and our residence for who knows how long. We finally got some food and the beds felt good after the impossible conditions on the train. I'm not sure how long we were housed there, but apparently it was about four to six weeks. What I do remember is every couple days having to report to a huge meeting hall that smelled suspiciously like a doctor's office or a hospital. Long lines of people stood in rows awaiting their turn to receive an injection against an outbreak of some disease or another. The sight of doctors, the equipment and children crying, made me faint every single time, way before it was my turn to receive a shot. It got so bad that the doctor would have me lay down before administering the shot knowing full well that I would wind up collapsed on the floor anyway. This fear of needles stayed with me for more than three decades. Finally, about fifteen of us, including Mothers friend Kate, were loaded onto a truck and driven to a small town named Utzenhofen. It was not even a city, because I saw no traffic lights or street car tracks. The bare farm land and huge forests bordered right on the outskirts of this hamlet. I heard they did have a school and even a hospital, neither of which I cared to ever visit. We hopped off the truck and stood almost ankle deep in mud, due to the spring thaw, much to my dismay, before getting assigned to various places to stay. But first I asked mother if we had arrived in Poland. None of us understood a single word the inhabitants were saying. "No, we are not in Poland," Kate replied with badly suppressed laughter. Poland was the only place I heard of that was a foreign place where people spoke differently. Turns out we were in Lower Bavaria, where the dialect is so different it sounded like an entirely other language. On this day I learned a new word: Refugee. We were refugees. I heard it murmured repeatedly by the small crowd that gathered, with the corners of their mouths turned down, as if it had a bad taste when spoken. I heard that word often from then on, the shape of the mouth never changed. Well, the four of us, including Kate, were directed quite a distance out of town, over a small bridge spanning a little brook, past seemingly never-ending forests and farm land, as well as several huge meadows. All of this was uphill, and it felt like we were walking a long time, maybe an hour? I felt we were definitely not welcome in that small town and send as far away as possible. Finally, we spotted a tiny, white Cape Cod style house. It was owned by a lady who had some chickens, ducks and a few rabbits for company, as well as the customary cat, that was on a perpetual hunt for field mice. I also spotted a goat and thought she would be a nice pet to play with. This poor woman was required, or ordered, to give us a roof over our heads, and that was exactly what we got: to sleep in the attic directly under the roof. Her living quarters on the ground floor consisted of one bedroom, a living room, kitchen and a rustic little outhouse a bit off to the side of the house. A round stone walled well was the only source of water and was only about twenty feet from the front door. We got the upstairs, which was basically the attic, which should have housed old pieces of furniture and other castoffs. Instead, about half of the space was filled with hay and straw for the animals. We also discovered there were no walls and no ceiling, just the beams that supported the roof. It was an entirely unfinished place. Mother hoped out loud to Kate the roof would not leak if it ever rained. By now it was April and still quite chilly, but there was no way to heat the attic. We did have a window at "our" end of the attic, the only source of light. It overlooked a small fenced in vegetable garden but leaning precariously out of the window and glancing to the right, we also got a better look at a rather large farm house some distance away. Together with several other buildings it formed a very large square surrounding a huge courtyard. This place consisting of only two buildings actually had a name, it was called Zapfl. I could hardly wait to explore the whole area, but first we had to try and make the bare attic somewhat inhabitable. We were given six foot long by three feet wide burlap sacks, that were filled with straw to be used as mattresses, and some blankets. Mother tried to make the place as homey as one possibly could, given the lack of furniture with the exception of one chair. The weather started to get nicer by the day and with that came some chores. It was my duty to sweep the entrance hallway with a straw broom, because with so many people traipsing in and out, a lot of dirt was being carried inside. The door was kept open most of the time, which was an invitation for the little critters to come in and sometimes relieve themselves in such comfortable surroundings. One day, in the midst of my sweeping, a small duckling was doing his, or her, dirty business in the hallway. All I wanted to do was to usher that fluff ball out of the house with the help of my broom. I took a swing and sent the poor thing flying, never realizing the power of my rather golf-like swing. It fell to the ground halfway between the front door and the well and did not attempt to get up. I ran quickly to check the little yellow cutie, but it lay dead. I was shocked, mad at myself and devastated at the same time, for I had killed a small living thing. For some reason I was not punished for that misdeed and think that is the reason I never forgot about it. The owner of the large nearby farm was supposed to supply us with necessary food items, but that never happened. He felt it was not his duty to help us unwanted refugees. While snarling the distasteful word at my brother and me, we were ordered off his property. Mother was definitely wrong in assuming that it would be better to send children for a hand-out. I asked her why we were treated with such hatred, after all, we were all Germans and should help each other in times of need. As it turns out it had all to do with religion and location. We came from the northeast, a mostly Lutheran region, where everyone spoke the high German language known as Hochdeutsch (high German), as taught in schools, while the south was predominantly catholic with a dialect that was completely foreign to us, as mentioned before. In feudal times the King of Prussia and the king of Bavaria must have really had a beef with each other, for until this day anyone born north of Bavaria is cynically called a Prussian by some folks. The passing of time and politics seems to have done little to educate narrow minds. So, this was it, we were treated like foreigners. Mother finally made the trek on foot to the little town of Utzenhofen, where we initially arrived, and got a written order from the mayor's office, which stated that food supplies to us were mandatory. In the meantime, my brother and I became quite adept at stealing anything we could eat. We helped ourselves to potatoes from their hidden storage place, as well as some eggs from the hen house, after we discovered a loose board on the back wall of the hen house. Our landlady's small vegetable garden yielded enough carrots, green beans and onions to share with us. In the meantime, brother and I explored the countryside. We roamed across fields and into the forests, which were dark, and with a little imagination it made me feel like I might come across Little Red Riding Hood and the bad wolf. Being a city child, I was surprised to find myself easily at one with nature and the solitude that came with it. One day I watched the farmers hired help mow a meadow to make hay for the animals, when I spotted a baby bunny, who almost was being chopped up by the heavy machine. I ran towards him to save his life, and to my surprise he let me pick him up. I guessed he was too young to have learned to fear humans. Mother gave her okay, which surprised me even more. She had gotten a bit mellower since her friend Kate came to live with us, possibly because of the adult conversations they shared. There was less time needed to bother with us children, the great outdoors became our playground. So, I carried the bunny to our attic, where I made a little bed of straw for him close to my bed. He seemed content, let me pet him and I was falling in love with this cute little creature. This seemed to work out fine, but a couple days later I awoke to find him in the makeshift bed with me. I suppose he wanted to feel the warmth of my body, so he had no problem hopping onto my floor level bed. Unfortunately, I must have rolled over and on top of him at some time during the night, crushing his poor little body flat as a potato pancake. My grief and feelings of guilt for ending his life so soon found no end. To make matters worse, I now felt like a double murderess. Kate finally convinced me that this was bound to happen sooner or later, because animals born to the wild were not meant to share a bed with people, therefore it was not my fault, just an accident. Yet in the recesses of my mind, I felt marked as a person who should not be allowed to ever have another pet.

Barely a few days later we awoke one morning to find the little house surrounded by gun carrying soldiers, wearing a type of uniform mother and Kate did not recognize. Both women tried to find out who they were, so mother asked in a normal voice "are you Germans", to which one soldier, who seemed to be in command, took a threatening stance and replied something in a foreign language. The situation seemed tense and some of the soldiers pointed their rifles at the window. By now Mother was very scared and decided we needed to give ourselves up to avoid any conflict. I was directed to take a white bed sheet, run downstairs and climb the fence, then tie the sheet to the pole that supported the clothes line. This, I found out, was the international sign of capitulation. No sooner was the sheet hung from the pole, the soldiers acted a bit relaxed, and some came into the house to conduct a search of every room and the attic. It turned out these were Hungarians, and we never did find out what side they fought on. The side of the Germans? They were quite friendly and gave my brother and me rides on their horses, which made me wonder why we did not hear them approach the house. But why wonder, as long as we were given rides and had some fun, which was rather short lived. I watched my mother being hoisted onto one of the horses, as she alternately protested and giggled nervously the whole time. They must soon have figured out she most likely had never been on a horse, and therefore tied her feet together with a rope under the horses' belly to prevent her from falling off. By now all of them were mounted and the horse my mother sat on received a flat handed slap on the rump from the leader of the group. The horse took off in a full gallop and my mother shrieked the whole time until all were out of sight and just a tiny cloud of dust was evidence that a group had departed in a hurry. I just stood there waiting for her to return, but after more than an hour or so passed, it was clear to me this may not happen for a while, and I felt she had been stolen from us. In the meantime, Kate did her best to take care of the three of us and after I don't know how many days had gone by, Mother returned on foot with a big box of food and a nice pair of leather boots for herself. She appeared in good spirits and told Kate that one of the soldiers, by the name of Tony, had fallen in love with her and wanted to marry and take her to Hungary when the war was over. She apparently did not feel the same way and told him to get lost, dumb ass. He was a bit persistent and always replied "Tony good, dumb ass." That phrase was repeated several times and caused hilarity for a few days, then he either got the hint or marching orders, but the Hungarians were gone as swiftly as they had arrived.

A few days had passed, and the adults enjoyed the serenity of the country, when one early morning the house was once more surrounded by soldiers. This time there was no doubt, these were German soldiers. At first, they acted less friendly than the Hungarians, but after a thorough search of the premises, which included piercing the piles of hay and straw with pitch forks, they treated us with less indifference. In fact, they got down right friendly, after finding out we were just poor refugees, who had to leave our home in the east before the Poles or the Russians got there. These soldiers looked so handsome in their uniforms that I secretly wished one of them would be my father, but no such luck. After spending just one night at the hay part of the attic they left as quickly as they had arrived, and I found myself missing their presence. In fact, it felt like a father had walked out of my life that day. Realizing that I knew absolutely nothing about my father, I decided to ask mother about him, but not until I knew she would be in an exceptionally good mood, some day. My thoughts were disrupted by some sporadic gun fire, and I wondered who was shooting whom. We never did find out, until decades later. The very next morning my mother was just about to shake her blanket out the window, when she let out a short gasp, followed by the now almost familiar words "are you Germans?" The house was once again surrounded by soldiers, with their guns drawn and ready to shoot. She repeated her question a second time only to see several soldiers raise their weapons and aiming them directly at the window. Kate had joined her at the window and muttered "these are definitely not Germans." Mother yelled to us kids to hang up the white sheet in a hurry. Karl-Heinz got to it first, climbed the fence and fastened the sheet just like I had done already twice before. In an instant they were all over the house searching every corner and stabbing the straw and hay with a pitchfork that was leaning against the wall next to the straw. At the same time a group disappeared into a large forest not far from the house. I don't know how much later, but suddenly we heard many shots being fired. I have never wanted to know who and how many were killed on that day. With all the excitement around him, my baby brother must have sensed the tension and started to cry hysterically. One somewhat portly soldier put his gun down and picked up the baby in the hopes he would stop crying, but Mother must have thought the child was being kidnapped. She lunged at the man while yelling for him to put down the baby. He just gently held her back with one outstretched arm, while rocking the baby, who actually stopped his wailing. I really don't know how, but it was determined these were Americans. After nothing threatening or nourishing was found in this house, they began to plan the next step, namely a visit to the huge farm house just one thousand or so feet down the dirt road. We did not see what happened, but as it got dark Karl-Heinz and I went to investigate. As we approached the entrance to the court yard we saw several fires. At first, I thought they were burning the place down, but then it became apparent these were cooking fires, about ten of them, with several soldiers busy getting meals done around each. We were spotted by one of the Americans and must have looked hungry, because we were immediately offered anything we wanted or needed. It felt like Christmas time. Bread, milk, butter, eggs and anything we could carry we hauled to "our" little house, and then Mother sent us back again for some meats, because she expected this good fortune to come to an end real soon. There was no sign of the farmer, his wife or any of their people. We suspected they were less than welcoming to the troops and were therefore just run off the place, but we got fresh milk every day for as long as the troop was there. Somehow over the past few days of exploring the area I must have gotten a cut or a thorn in my right thumb, which resulted in a fierce infection. I developed a huge blister filled with puss, and the pain was severe when touched. Being right-handed, I was not able to do anything, nor did I go to the farm house to snoop what the Americans were doing. One of them came to the house to check on us, when he noticed my dilemma. I somehow trusted him when he checked my swollen thumb, but I did not want him near me with that sterilized needle to pop the blister. He won. As I lay kicking and whimpering on my back, he simply wedged my wrist between his knees and opened the blister, squeezed the puss out thereby instantly relieving me of the pain. A huge bandage served as my badge of bravery and after it healed a small triangular scar was visible, which would stay with me forever. The Americans were really moved in at the farm, killing and roasting chickens almost every evening, enjoying some beverages and music provided by one of their own on a harmonica. At night, returning to our little house, my brother and I had to duck into the gully beside the road to avoid being seen by the light of tracer bullets being shot to burst into bright light above the road. I had no idea why this was done, but it seemed dangerous and we ducked for cover in the ditch along the dirt road every time. I wondered if this was meant to light the way back to the house. Maby? Pretty soon the Americans moved on, the farmers moved back from wherever they had gone to, and things got quiet, but just for a short time. One afternoon we heard a plane, and before any of us realized what was happening, the plane opened fire on "our" little house. As the bullets tore through the roof we ran as fast as possible outside. In the distance we saw the plane turn and head back in our direction. Mother shouted not to stay in the open, but to run under a huge tree to the right, just about one hundred feet away. The pilot must have seen us running and headed straight for the tree, shooting a barrage of bullets that missed their mark, because we stood pressed against the huge trunk on the far side, away from the attack. Our objective was to run into the forest that was still several hundred yards away, but there were two more trees equally spaced, that we could use for cover. To our disbelief the plane made yet another turn as we ran even faster to reach the second tree. Again, we huddled close to it on the side away from the approaching airplane as it strafed the area, barely missing us. At this time, we did not even look, we knew that pilot would not give up and come at us again. As soon as the plane passed over us, we headed for the third and last tree. Mother was lagging a bit behind because she carried the baby, who was now about nine months old. The field we had to cross was not at all an even surface, but with many indentations from having been plowed and holes dug by woodchucks. As expected by the two women, the plane once again turned and attacked the third tree, missing his mark as we hoped. We ran with our last bit of energy, but propelled by fear, into the dark forest we hoped would save us. I guess I was a fast runner and first to enter the forest, then came to a halt about fifty feet into what I hoped was a place of safety. Dropping to my knees, face on the backs of my hands, which rested on the mossy forest floor, and with my butt in the air, I tried to catch my breath and hoped the others were right behind me. There was total silence, the plane did not pursue the little band of two women and three children any more. The silence lasted perhaps a minute or two, then was broken by bursts of first halted, then hilarious laughter emanating from Kate. Mother murmured that her friend just lost her mind, but Kate pointed her index finger in my direction, making mother look at me. Now my mother started to laugh out loud as well, as I remained in my original position. It turns out my dress had slipped up to expose my panties, which displayed a perfectly round hole exposing my butt hole. That sight evoked laughter from the two adults and thereby much needed release of the tension and fear accumulated over the last minutes. After we felt it was safe to do so, we returned to the house and found our landlady, who saw no reason to run since she survived the attack on the ground floor of the house. She was making a pot of coffee that was welcomed and enjoyed by the adults. Many years later I learned it was common practice for pilots returning from a mission not to land with any leftover ammunition. In this case they were either British or American pilots, who used this time of returning to their base to just shoot at anything, like buildings, animals and of course people. Living in the attic several months had disclosed some leaks on rainy days and nights. There was an array of pots and bowls arranged to catch the drips of water, each vessel making its own sound as a concert of strange music was being played. But now the roof was riddled with bullet holes as well, that made habitation impossible. Over the next few nights, we could see the stars through each bullet hole, plus there were not enough pots and pans in the entire house to catch the water when it rained, to sleep here was not feasible any longer. The mayor of the nearby town was notified to find more suitable accommodations for the refugees, it was time to move.

We were assigned a very small room with a potbellied stove and two bunk beds in an once charming, wooden cabin, which was referred to as the hunting lodge. Since there were also two farm houses in reasonably close proximity, this was actually a tiny town named Schwierz. Who knew that three not very large houses close to nothing could be considered a town, but wait, did I forget so soon that the previous place consisted only of one farm and one little house was named Zapfl? This new place was a one hour walk, all again up hill, from the small city where we were dumped by a truck months ago. Said hunting lodge, whose owner was rumored to live in Nuremberg, was definitely a step up from our former residence, but not by much. Calling it a hunting lodge was giving it more credit than it deserved. It was really not more than a cabin that consisted of a rather large living room and a kitchen on the ground floor. An outside stairway on the side of the building led to a big, dormitory style bedroom with rows of wooden cots on the two long sides of the room. The upstairs was always locked, and we were only allowed to use the kitchen that came outfitted with one set of bunk beds. I had to share the upper bunk with my brother, Mother was in the lower bunk and the baby brother was comfortably sleeping in his carriage. The first night I fell from the upper bunk and hit my head on the cast iron potbellied stove. I'm glad to have survived, but I am pretty sure that I had a concussion. Mothers one hour walk to the mayor resulted in us getting the big room on the ground floor, just a few days later. We could hardly believe our good luck, the room was at least three times the size of the former room, which was really meant to be just a kitchen. It had real beds, a two-burner hot plate for proper cooking, as well as a table and chairs. I guess we only deserved one room, from the day we moved to the big room the kitchen was no longer available to us and locked tight.

On our first night we were welcomed by a multitude of mice. While lying flat on my back that night I actually felt a mouse running across my chest. I was in awe of my own reflexes as I grabbed that mouse and flung it to the floor. Mother was intent on winning the war against the mice with the help of some traps we found. These little pests were obviously residing here long before we interrupted their happy home. We could actually hear them running along the narrow shelves, situated just a couple feet below the ceiling and encircling the entire room, during the night. I imagined the shelves held many trophies after hunting parties. If that was not enough, we also found out that each bed was infested by bed bugs, plus what bed bugs were up to in the dark and all through the night. They actually love human blood, which I thought was a real creepy thought. As soon as it was dark and we lay in our beds, the bugs started to gently nibble our skin and sucked blood from our extremities. Now Mother was on a more aggressive war path. Next morning promised to be a beautiful day ahead, so all mattresses were taken out in the fresh air. With a rag soaked in kerosene, every mattress was wiped along all seams and possible hiding places. This was a very time-consuming task, and after Mother was through debugging, all mattresses were left outside for the rest of the day to get rid of the smell of kerosene. The next few nights proved this method appeared to have been somewhat successful. I had my fingers crossed, just in case.

Over the next couple of days, I was able to explore our new home and surrounding areas. The first thing I noticed was the absence of a bathroom facility or toilet, not even an outhouse. The metal bucket in a small room at the rear of the house, only to be entered from the outside, confirmed its allocated use. A nail on a wall with cut squares of newspaper told me it was not for reading.

Squatting over the bucked to relieve oneself proved to be very uncomfortable and demanded a certain amount of balance, not to mention aim. When full it had to be carried up an incline behind the cabin and a small distance into the forest. There I discovered an already dug ditch for disposal. This made me realize that we really were in the wild backwoods of the country. That ditch was actually, as it turned out, very strategically dug right between two trees that stood about four feet apart. A plank of wood was then nailed so as to connect the trees about one and a half feet off the ground at the back side, and another plank connected the front of the trees at about three feet high. I recognized this at once as an outdoor, though crude, toilet. The low plank was for sitting on and the higher one for holding onto, so you would not fall backwards into the ditch. A rather large nail on one of the trees confirmed this, even though there was no toilet paper or cut up newspaper on the nail. The next thing missing in the cabin was a source of running water. The nearest drinking water was a small spring about 300 yards away from the cabin, but much closer to the farm houses, with clear, cold water bubbling out of a cement enclosed hole in the ground. This constantly flowing water formed a cute little brook, which then joined a bigger brook that flowed past the cabin, but that water was not for drinking. Instead, it served my brother and me as a wading pool on hot summer days, since it was only about two feet deep. He and I had the job of getting water from the spring many times a day, using two enamels two-liter pitchers, walking back and forth in rain or shine. In the winter months the path to the spring was covered with ice from spilling part of the water while hurrying to get out of the cold.

It was time to check out the two modest farm houses. The one closest to us sat on a more elevated ground with a bigger barn in front of it, and they were supposed to supply us with the usual food items to survive. They were not thrilled by that but were less hostile than the much larger farm at our previous location. There were only three people at this house, a man and his wife, her name was Franziska, and an old man, obviously the father of one of them. Karl-Heinz and I called him grandpa, but not to his face at first. There were no children around. The other and smaller house stood about two hundred feet perpendicular to the first house, with a very unfriendly man and his adult daughter. They had a large German shepherd dog tied to a long chain, who went aggressive as all get out if one of us set one foot on their property. That chain was fastened to a wooden rail so the dog could patrol the house from one end to the other. Needless to say, we stayed clear of that place.

Mother must have felt it was time for her two offspring to continue their basic education and registered us at the nearest school, which was in the town of Utzenhofen, where we first arrived, an approximately one hour walk away. I really do not remember much of our first day of schooling, but very vividly recall many of the local kids calling us refugees, refugees at the end of each class, but never in front of a teacher. At the end of the school day, once outside the building, they chased us down the street, picking up stones and pebbles which they hurled at us. I did not see any such ammunition in my immediate area, but I spotted a rather firm looking pile of horse poop. Without hesitation I picked up some of the fist sized poop in each hand, because they looked like perfect weapons, and fired away in their direction. I have no clue if any of these hit the mark, but those kids were momentarily stunned enough for us to run out of town. We must have looked a bit disheveled and smelled some too. After Mother heard what had happened, she decided we were smarter than those country bumpkins for now and did not have to go back to school again. She actually said we were smarter than those dumb farm brats, therefore our first day of school was also our last, for the next two years. That decision suited Brother and me just fine.

Food was always scarce, so mother decided to sell off a couple of my best dresses that were, in her words, starting to get a little small for me anyway. I recall one that was made of dark blue velvet with colorful beads sown in the shape of little ducks across the chest. The next dress was of a shiny pink material and every bit as fancy as the first, something the farmers had not seen before. I really hated to part with them, because they were presents from Mothers rather well-off aunts and uncles, being I was the first child of my generation borne into the family. But we needed food, so Mother walked far to find a farm family with a little girl, who were willing to pay with sufficient food, including bread, butter and eggs. From now on I had only one or two dresses left to wear, so I had to share my brother's limited wardrobe. I did not feel badly about that, his shorts were real comfortable with the few tops I had left. Unfortunately, one day I discovered that I could not remove my red and white striped sweater. I tried pulling it over my head, but when I tugged hard, I felt a bit of pain in my neck. Mother took one look at me and diagnosed my problem as having a case of the mumps. The only way to remove the sweater was to unravel it, cutting it off was out of the question. She found the beginning of the cotton thread at the bottom and started to dismantle my best, and only, sweater. I turned round and around myself as she produced a red and a white ball of yarn to be turned into another garment at a later date. I never did see another sweater or anything else made from what I thought was my yarn.

I did not know until several years later why mother had to leave so suddenly that summer. She took a few items of clothing and Lothar in his baby carriage, and went hitch hiking deeper into Bavaria, right to the border between Germany and Austria, to see her two younger sisters Brigitte and Charlotte. It was summertime and Karl-Heinz and I were now in Franziska and her husband's care.

The first evening meal with them and "grandpa" was most unusual for us. We sat around a table that had a soup spoon by each seat. Brother and I patiently waited for the plates, but instead a very big bowl containing a bread soup was placed in the middle of the table. Brother and I looked at each other as the three adults proceeded to pick up their spoons and dip into that bowl and ate. I was shocked and appalled at the sight of the three of them dipping their spoons into the same bowl. I have never forgotten the feeling that we have joined a family totally lacking any table etiquette. We had waited for some plates to be placed before us. This informal type of dining had to be gotten used to, I thought, when Franziska urged us to start eating. I tried my best to dip my spoon into an area of the bowl where no one had yet dipped their spoon into, of fear there might be some saliva present. Karl-Heinz was not that picky, he enjoyed the freedom of the slurping. By the end of the meal there was a trail of little spills from the bowl to each person's space, and I watched as Franziska very vigorously scrubbed the table after the utensils were removed. I was impressed at her apparent cleanliness, because Mother was absolutely never enthused by the fine art of cleaning or doing dishes. Lunches were usually thick slices of home baked bread and home cured meats or cheese. At first, we were still sleeping at the cabin, but one afternoon we inadvertently almost started a forest fire. After roaming around in the forest, we got a bit hungry and decided to roast a couple potatoes that we dug out of the edge of a large field. We build a fire, but it was too close to a pine tree. To be truthful, the fire was right under the tree, and as the flames got higher the tree suddenly was aflame. We heard a bell ring in the distance, obviously a fire alarm, and knew immediately we were in deep trouble. We did not stick around to witness the fire being put out but headed to our "tree house" at the edge of an adjoining forest. This was actually quite a high look-out for hunters during hunting season that we made our own. We had a small stash of carrots and radishes as emergency rations that came in handy on just such occasions. That evening we returned to the cabin but found it had been securely locked. We knew we had to face the consequences from our earlier adventure.

From now on we had to sleep at the farm house and do some light chores as well. Karl-Heinz was in charge of the cows while grazing, which made me laugh, because he was only six years old and a bit small for his age. My chore was to keep the flock of geese together, no small feat, because they were all going in different directions. At least the cows stayed in one spot, but for the geese I had to use a long stick to keep them together. Finally, I got tired and took a chance to lay in the grass and stare at the clouds, thinking about the joy of our newfound freedom away from Mothers moods and temper outbursts. What I did not know was the fact that what goes into a goose comes out the other end in no time at all. The field of grass was dotted with their poop, much of which now stuck to my back side. After herding them back into their pen I simply sat up to just a little above my waist in the brook and cleaned up as best I could. While sitting in the water I discovered a bunch of polliwogs, not yet frogs, swimming around me.

They were great fun to watch and handle, making me forget that we had absolutely no toys to play with.

Early one Sunday morning Franziska must have thought it necessary to take me to church with her. There was no breakfast, she had me dressed up and we walked and walked to town. I mentioned I would have liked something to eat before leaving, but she informed me that Catholics do not eat before church. We sat in the front pew and at some point, the priest was swinging a round metal object on a chain from left to right repeatedly. At each change of direction, a little white cloud of smoke emerged from that object. The smell made me feel uneasy at first, then it reminded me of a doctor's office visit, and I started to feel real sick. Finally, I tugged on Franziska's arm and told her I was not feeling well. She told me to go outside, but as I began to walk towards the door I felt as if I was swaying while making my way to the door, which appeared to me like a big black hole that I needed to enter. By now I felt very weak and ready to collapse. I barely reached the door and somehow stumbled outside, when my legs gave way, and I fainted right at the church door. I awoke to people stepping over me and continue on their way as if I was not there, or worse, as if I was a mere pebble that they just stepped over. Until that moment I had never felt so alone, and since Franziska sat in the front pew, she came out last. After asking what happened, she helped me up and we took the long walk home and had a good, although delayed breakfast. She never took me to church again, I thanked her silently for sparing me that unpleasant activity.

It seems Mother had taken Lothar to my aunt Charlotte to be taken care of by her, while Mother was going to the hospital for an operation, something about an infection or cyst on the ovaries. I did not know what that was, but told it is a female thing. After having Lothar, who was now one year old, tucked away safe and sound, she had made her way back to Utzenhofen and the hospital near where we two kids were. There was just one problem, this was a Catholic hospital, and my mother was Lutheran, in other words a Protestant. So, the hospital refused to administer any help or procedure for her, in fact they did not allow her to enter the building. She collapsed on the sidewalk, someone called the ambulance, and the poor driver did not know what to do with her. He did go to the mayor of Utzenhofen who ordered the hospital to take her in and perform the necessary procedures for her condition. All of this was not known to me or my brother, and I wonder if Franziska and her husband had any such knowledge. None of us had known that Mother had made her way back to Utzenhofen by hitch hiking and languished at the hospital there.

Summer was gone, the weather turned colder, and still no word of Mothers whereabouts or when she would return. On Christmas Eve day, just after lunch, we had an unexpected visit from two nuns, who informed us in a rather matter of fact way that my mother had died. The shock was clearly visible on Franziska's and her husband's face. I imagine they were at a loss as to what would have to be done next about Karl-Heinz and me. To my utter surprise I was not at all devastated by the news of Mothers death. I don't think I really believed it. In fact, I did not feel anything at all. How is this possible, I thought, I should be crying my eyes out? Somehow, I did find a reason to justify my stoic behavior, namely that I did not quite believe this news, and secondly, I had spent more years with Mother and her many temper outbursts than Karl-Heinz did. While he was having a well ordered and loving time with Mommy Deen, I had to endure physical and mental punishment for being an unwanted burden, who ruined her freedom and the chance to do whatever she pleased. The next day I overheard the husband and wife mention that they would like to keep the boy, my brother, but did not want the girl, meaning me. An orphan without a home, hmm, at least I knew I came from Goerlitz and Omi would take care of me. No need to worry now. The next few days were spent in half silence, none of us knew how we were supposed to act or feel. I do not even remember if Karl-Heinz felt any sense of loss. Four days after the initial nuns visit, we had another visit from the same, or were these two different nuns? At least I thought they might have been different, even though they all looked alike with their head to toe black habit and only a white sort of collar. But this time they informed us that my mother was still alive, but just barely. How could she be dead on Christmas Eve and alive four days later? Do nuns not know the difference between a dead and an alive person? By now I was very confused and not trusting what the next news might bring. Adults don't seem to be all that smart, at any rate, the inhabitants of this farm were happy. Not that they jumped up and down for joy, but I could see by the expression on their faces that for now at least no plans had to be made about what to do with us kids. I remembered what the farmer had said about keeping my brother and thought well, now you don't get to keep him and split us up. I did feel just a little bit sad for the couple, because they had no children of their own.

Brother and I tried to have some fun in the snow with an enormous sled we found on the farm property. It was meant to be pulled by one or two horses. It had a long pole attached to the front to which usually one or two horses would be hitched. I don't know how we managed to get the sled to the top of the hill next to the farm, but we sure worked hard at it and finally did it. It was clear from the start this was going to be for one ride only. Because the farm was already located half way up that hill, we knew right away we could not move that large sled all the way up from the very bottom. After that hard work and a short pause, we gave the sled a mighty push, jumped on top and we were off on the best ride ever. The sheer size and weight of that sled made it pick up speed. It felt like we flew down the incline, across the walk way that led to the cabin, across the not entirely frozen brook and straight into a huge bramble bush. The pole disappeared completely into the bush, but we were spared any injury following that sudden stop and just walked away, leaving the sled where it was.

Winter was over, April and my eighth birthday passed without any mention, but the farmer was out of straw for the cows bedding. I was assigned the seemingly easy task of chopping a big pile of Christmas tree branches on a tree stump that served as a chopping block, into small bits with a hatchet. This could be a fun job, and after a couple branches lay chopped to bits on the floor of the barn and all around me, I picked up speed. I guess my enthusiasm got the best of me, until I saw the tip of my left index finger fly in an arc onto the pile of green in front of me. To my surprise there was no immediate pain, but I had the absolute urge to look for, and find, that missing piece of my finger so I could stick it back on. At this point I looked for the first time at my finger and saw blood running over my hand. In order not to lose too much blood I held my arm high and started to feel faint. Once that feeling came over me, there was no stopping it, so I walked out of the barn and for no reason known to me, headed for the cabin as if someone was there to take care of my wound. Half way there I passed out and have no recollection about what happened to me after that. My fingertip grew back eventually, but I do have a fine line to remind me of what happened, and I got no more jobs involving a hatchet.

Karl-Heinz and I promised Franziska not to get into any more trouble if we could sleep again in our cabin, but we will show up for our meals. We enjoyed our freedom to the fullest by exploring the forests around us, and occasional rest breaks at our hunters look out, high up in a tall tree. Sometimes we climbed up the tallest tree around when we felt a bit lost, just to orientate ourselves and find a way out and back to the cabin. We also discovered that it was much easier to climb up a tree than it was to come down again, which can present a problem when suddenly nature calls while you are still high off the ground and can't get down fast enough. I never confessed to my brother that at least on one such occasion I was a bit scared of being lost in the forest forever. The first night on our own in the cabin seemed like we were not getting much sleep. Our single beds were separated by a night table on which stood a candle as our only source of light. As soon as we got under the covers and blew out the candle, we both felt like there was something in bed with us. I lit the candle again and flipped the blanket off me to see what it was. As the light found the sheet, I saw small bugs running for cover. We knew instantly that the bed bugs had not been entirely eradicated. At once we became hunters and proceeded to look for a suitable weapon. Mother had a small sewing kit, so we decided that a darning needle would be a good spear against these small, but bloodthirsty critters. The plan was to flip the covers back real quick, then stab as many as we could with the needles. This sounded like it could be fun as we had no toys to play with. It worked. After I had the first one on my spear, I did not know what to do with it. I looked it over and saw it was full of my blood.

There was no water handy to drown it and setting it free outside was not an option. They would only return, so we decided that death by fire was the only way to get rid of them. We did not have to build a fire; the candle was good enough. Time after time we covered ourselves until we felt a few bites, then flipped the cover back and stabbed as many of these pests as fast as we could. Usually we just got one, sometimes two, because they are fast as lightning. Then we held them with the needle over the flame of the candle until they went puff and exploded and were gone. This hunting game went on until we got tired and fell asleep without caring how much of our blood they sucked out. We spent a couple more nights like the last in the cabin but got tired of fighting the bugs and went back to sleep at the farm house. The beds were softer there and the goose down comforters felt warm and luxurious. We also found grandpa was very hard of hearing and we were allowed to yell instead of softly talking out of respect for our Elders. Every few days he would wander around the nearby meadows and pick a variety of leaves, berries and flowers, which he put into a perpetually steeping enamel bowl on the tiled oven. Every day he drank that brew he called tea, then just added more water to the bowl. I found it amazing how he knew what to pick, he believed it helped to keep him healthy, and whenever he offered me a cup of his magic tea, I drank it gladly.

One day, while Karl-Heinz and I were at one of our favorite spots in the forest, we heard an unfamiliar voice calling me and my brother's name. It turned out she was Mothers sister Charlotte, whom we had not met before. She had my baby brother Lothar in her care. The sole reason she showed up was to find out what happened to our mother, her oldest sister, because she had not heard from her sister since she dropped off Lothar just about a year ago. Franziska informed Charlotte about what transpired over the winter, specifically at Christmas time, so our new aunty went to the hospital to see for herself what was going on. The report after her return was not a good one, in fact she was shocked at seeing Mothers face, which was so white that she looks like she was made of wax. She was delirious as well as in and out of consciousness and did not recognize that her sister or anyone else was present. The room itself was kept at an absolute bare minimum, as far as furniture or any decoration was concerned. The walls were a stark white, with only a metal bed and one nightstand, and one wall was adorned with a rather large crucifix. Aunt Lotte, as we called her, got along very well with our host couple. They spent many hours in the evenings discussing the war and Lotte's flight from Berlin, where she survived multiple bombings and the horrendous sights of many dead civilians. She finally left Berlin and headed per thumb to live with another sister, our aunt Brigitte, whom we also had not met before, and lived in the Bavarian town of Burghausen, right on the border to Austria. During about a month's time, while Aunt Lotte stayed with my brother and me, we housed in the cabin, which she sprayed with something to get rid of some more bed bugs and had a relatively good time. I did wish she could stay longer, but she had to get back to Burghausen and care for Lothar, because Aunt Brigitte had a small child of her own, plus three children from her husband's first marriage. After Aunt Lotte left, we enjoyed our carefree existence as summer slowly eased into fall. A couple months went by with no particular routine I can remember.

One fall day I saw an older woman approach, using two canes to steady her slow walk. She wore a kerchief and a jacket, even though it was not yet cold out. We lived in such an isolated area that anything out of the usual was observed with great interest, in fact with just good old fashioned and deliberate nosy interest. As the lady got closer a hint of recognition on my part made my eyes almost bug out. I was actually watching my mother approach and thinking what has happened to her. She appeared much older than her years. There was no time for a long greeting, it was immediately urgent to get her to lay down in the cabin as soon as possible. I helped her undress carefully, because I had no clue if she had any bandages or only band aids on her. Once she got carefully, and with great effort into her bed she started to relax and fell asleep for a while. After she woke up, I thought she would be hungry, but instead she showed me what needed to be done first. After moving the covers off herself and lifting her nightgown I was ready to faint at first. Because the sight of two tubes protruding on either side of her, right where the thigh meets the rump, was almost too much for me to handle. It was now my job to help her clean the areas where a puss like liquid oozed out of the tubes. Until this moment I had never realized how tough Mother had to be to walk over two hours from the hospital, mainly uphill and tubes protruding from her body to the cabin. I always knew she was strong willed and tough, one smack from her would confirm that. But to walk that distance in her condition was only due to sheer willpower on her part. Once the tubes stopped leaking, they could be removed and the healing phase begin, but I truly do not remember when and who removed the tubes. I just know it was not done by me, thank goodness. I suppose she must have returned to the hospital for that procedure. Frankly, I do not want to remember that part. She started to get out of bed and move around the cabin a little more each day, but tired soon. One day I wanted to make her a nice breakfast, however, we had no eggs. I had seen some pigeons fly in and out of the farmers hay barn, so I figured there might be something I could use. Sure enough, there were some cute little eggs in their nest, so I decided to take only two and fry them up for my mother. The plan worked; I served her the eggs with a piece of bread with butter. She took a look at the cute sunny side up eggs and asked suspiciously what kind of eggs they were. Without hesitation I told her they were from midget hens I had discovered at the farm, and they would taste real good. She bought that story and I was proud of myself as I watched her enjoying the breakfast I had prepared. I had no remorse about telling her such a bold-faced lie. She seemed to feel better as the days and weeks flew by, and winter was just around the corner. With the arrival of the first snowfall, we were excited at first, then it just kept coming day after day, it was unending and we were stuck inside the cabin for what seemed like years. The snow was over three feet deep when it finally stopped and there was no snow shovel available to us. During those many days while stuck in the cabin, Mother had started to tell how she survived at the hospital. I told her about the two visits from the nuns and how the farmers were concerned as to what would happen next. Mother told us that after the operation her condition worsened, her body was wracked with infections that kept on worsening from day to day. When she started to hallucinate, it appeared she was not going to survive. She was removed from the ward with many other patients to a room of her own, and it was anticipated she would die within a few days. In her delirium she saw the large crucifix as the grim reaper, who was beckoning her to follow him. She did not want to do that, because she had children to take care of. Really? That statement belied her real feelings about kids I thought. The saying that children should be seen but not heard was not at all what she believed, instead she would have preferred to not have any at all. This was not just my assumption, but I overheard her mention that sentiment to her close girlfriend Kate, who had left Bavaria to try and find her husband in northern Germany. But I was listening to her story with great interest. Anyway, she did not want to keep seeing the reaper standing at the foot end of her bed, so she turned herself around, so that her head was now at the foot end. While she was telling this to us, I actually admired her strong will and determination.

The weather had turned nice, Karl-Heinz and I were taking turns again schlepping water from the spring. Mother was making the bed and told me to stir the breakfast soup made of water, flower and a little milk, to which I replied, just a minute. At that very moment the soup started to boil over and Mother was as quick as lightening by the stove, stirring and in an instant, I felt the pain of the wooden implement straight out of the hot liquid striking me in the face. My left cheek, just below the eye, was burning and water ran down my face. I had expected it to be blood, but only water, or were they tears, flowed towards my chin and dripped onto my top. I ran out of the cabin and into the forest to recover and feel sorry for and console myself. I knew at once SHE was back to her same old ill-tempered self. Later that day I returned to the cabin and Mother looked at me and asked what happened to my cheek. I felt like kicking her, or at the very least scream at her. Did she not remember, or want to remember, what took place earlier that day? I had always suspected that she was not all there mentally, in fact I suspected she was bat shit nuts. Could she that easily forget or just block out what she did? The crescent shaped scar remained on my face well into my late teens, but by the time I was in my early twenties the scar started to fade ever so slowly. Soon there was no longer a visual reminder of that day, except when I got a bit over heated through sport and my face turned red, I could still see a clear trace of the outline of the object she used on my face. Yet I could never forget that incident. While walking across the meadow earlier I found a dead frog and gave some thought of cutting him open. I was curious how his heart would look, could I even identify it? Before he started to smell I performed the operation and decided right there and then that I could never be a doctor. I found what I thought to be his heart and took it with me wrapped in a leaf. Back at the cabin I placed it on the window sill in the sun for no reason other than to let it dry out.

    I was outside when Mother called to me and asked with some interest what this thing on the sill was. I proudly proclaimed that this was the heart of a frog. I saw her eyes roll to the top of her head and she fell back in a faint with a big thud. I ran quickly inside and placed a wet cloth on her forehead, then ran away fast and thought to myself I got even for many things bad in my past. I also knew there would be a beating in the not so distant future, I might as well be prepared for that. This time I would have deserved a beating, but I am happy to report that nothing was even mentioned, per chance she was too weak to dole out punishment after having passed out.

After two years with Aunt Lotte, my little brother Lothar rejoined our family. He was the cutest looking three-year-old with a mop of curly golden blond hair that Mother could hardly get a comb through, plus the fact that he hated to stand still to have his hair combed. She did notice that he kept on scratching his head, which at first looked cute, but finally discovered he had head lice. Well, it was not long before my head was inundated with those pests, and I could actually feel them running around as if my head was their playground. Her instant solution was to wash my hair with kerosene and rinse with vinegar. That worked fine on me but could hardly be done to the little guy. Off she went with him on the long walk to Utzenhofen to see a barber, perhaps a haircut followed by a good wash would help the situation. At their return I could hardly believe my eyes, because my beautiful baby brother looked like an old bald mini man. They had found it necessary to shave his head. Because he was always scratching his head, it caused his scalp to form scabs, under which the lice would lay their eggs, therefore perpetuating the infestation. A salve applied daily was supposed to get rid of the scabs. That was the end of his curly hair, it grew back still blond, but straight.

Always asking for certain foods from the farmer was bothersome and somewhat demeaning, so Mother decided to plant a vegetable garden. The cabin had enough space and good soil, but I have no idea where she got seeds to plant string beans, carrots, radishes and other veggies in neat rows. The farmer's chickens were running around loose in the entire area, including visits to mother's garden, where one decided to retrieve the seeds Mother just planted. This was not going unpunished. The entire property of the cabin was secured by a chain link fence, and along the inside of the fence stood evenly spaced evergreens. This provided privacy and pleasing looking surroundings. Karl-Heinz and I were ordered to help her catch that wayward chicken, which should make a nice dinner and a good soup. The plan was to chase the bird into a corner and the three of us would attempt to catch it. That part went without much problem, but the chicken made quite a racket and we thought the farmer would hear this for sure. We quickly made our way to the rear of the cabin and into the little room where the infamous bucket was, as well as a chopping block we used often to split wood logs for heating in winter. Until now Mother held the chicken by its sides with the wings securely pressed to its body. Now what, I thought. Surely the bird will not do us the favor and die for us of natural causes. No, Mother had a plan again. She would have us hold the poor bird on the chopping block while she would wield the hatchet and end its short life with one swift chop. I wished there was an easier way to do this, but we had no pistol to shoot it quickly and using a knife did not sound any easier. Karl-

Heinz had the honor to hold the chicken just like Mother did and place it on the chopping block, but it would not hold its head still to receive a quick chop. I was elected to grab the head and stretch the neck out a bit so Mother could have a clear swing. That theory sounded pretty good and on the count of three that bird would meet a fast demise. At count two I happened to look up at Mother, who held the hatchet in both hands high over her head. But to my horror I saw that her eyes were tightly shut. How could she possibly see what she was doing with closed eyes? I feared losing my whole hand and by the time I heard the count of three, I had just the bird's beak between my right thumb and index finger. In that instant as the hatchet came down, I had my eyes closed as well. I think I remember hearing the bird let out one last squawk and then brother and I let go of the bird at the same time. To our amazement it took off running through the door with the head hanging just by a piece of skin the hatchet missed. We watched transfixed as it ran in circles while the blood trail marked its path. After what seemed like a very long time it fell dead to the ground, but I was still unable to move for a few more seconds. It was now up to Mother on how to deal with a dead chicken. She plucked the feathers out, but there were still many small ones, too small to be plucked. She decided to burn them off over a low gas flame. Unfortunately, this left many sooty stains, so she gave the bird a nice bath with soap and tepid water, followed by a few rinses in cold water. By now the biggest pot available had been filled with water and the clean bird, minus some of its guts, was lowered into it, along with some stuff like onions and carrots, to make it a soup. All this was boiling nicely when suddenly a slightly subdued mini explosion disrupted the silence. The three of us ran into the kitchen and stared at the simmering pot and watched in amazement as some small green bits, some worms and various seeds rose to the top. Obviously, Mother had forgotten to open and clean out the chicken's stomach, so whatever it ate was now swimming on top of the alleged broth. I tried hard but could not eat one spoon full of that, I was barely able to have some of the white meat. Mother just laughed at my disgust towards the polluted broth and remarked there would just be more for her to enjoy, and she did.

I was still the proud owner of my pocket knife and always curious about life in general, and what made things tick. To find the secret of life I had to find something to dissect, something bigger than just a frog. I did find a dead deer in the forest and thought about how to open its chest. I was able to talk my brother into helping me drag this rather large animal out of the forest and towards the only road leading towards the next town to the right, and towards the cabin to the left. Just as we reached the road, we heard a wagon and some voices approaching. It was the not so friendly farmer with his daughter atop a hay wagon pulled by two oxen. We hid at once behind some bushes and as soon as the oxen saw the dead deer at the side of the road they got frightened and started to run out of control. Brother and I did not stick around to observe the little stampede any further, yet we did hear many swear words as the wagon disappeared from view. We also abandoned the carcass as I realized that the little pocket knife was not going to do the job. I sincerely doubted that it would even be able to penetrate the tough hide of the deer.

It had started to rain in the afternoon and did not stop when it was time to go to bed. It was still pouring the next morning and all day, and the next day and the next. The huge meadow in front of the cabin was situated at least three or four feet lower than the ground our cabin stood on, but Mother was showing some concern about all the water that was now covering the entire meadow. It looked like we lived close to a giant lake, and it still kept on pouring day and night for at least around thirty-six days, or more. We actually saw a row boat with three men who came to see if we were all still alive and above water. Because of the mountainous terrain there was enough runoff from this flood as not to be life threatening, but it took a long time for the area to dry out again.

For some inexplicable reason mother was of the belief that the East-West border of Germany was only temporary. She tried to be in touch with her mom mainly to find out if it was safe to return to our home town, but communication was hard and slow to come by. Summer was coming to an end, so she had decided not to spend another winter in these rather spartan conditions. Besides, we kids had no schooling at all for over two and a half years and she realized we missed too much to be at the grade level in accordance with our age. At this point I am nine years old and do not exactly cherish any memories of the approximately half year in first grade of schooling I had so far. The few months of first grade, before we became refugees, were a bit frightening. My teacher was a Mrs. Voigt, who wore her steely gray hair pulled back in a bun at the nape of her neck. Not only did she look strict, but she was also strict. Her favorite item was a skinny bamboo stick, which she carried constantly and smacked her desk with when she heard the slightest sound. If one of us were to whisper, or heaven forbid giggle out loud, the punishment was painful. The offender had to come to the front of the class and hold the right hand out straight with palm facing up. She then raised the stick and landed a hit across the finger tips with such speed, the air whistled as the weapon came down hard. For each time you dared to pull your hand away you got an extra hit, after which the finger tips swelled to twice the size and it stung as if attacked by a wasp. I know about that first hand, because I was the recipient of that treatment for daring to giggle one day. I was thrilled when schools closed and became barracks for soldiers, and not at all excited to go to school again, after the most recent experience at the hands of the farm kids. Most of all I knew I would miss the freedom I had come to appreciate, especially while Mother was in the hospital.

By the time we left Zapfl it was a cold February day. And I remember a very short sleep on the hard wood floor of the train, while wondering why we are once again traveling during the coldest month. It appears there were no seats to be had but at least there were no more attacks from low flying planes. I was so looking forward to see my dear Oma again after all this time, and I was truly overjoyed at the prospect to see her at our arrival in Goerlitz, at the train station. The train pulled into the station way too slow. Patience has never been a strong virtue for me, so I grew just a little anxious to get my welcome hug after my brothers. Naturally Lothar got most of the attention, because he was only six months old when we had left and was now a three year old. The first few nights were spent at Oma's apartment and everything seemed so hectic. Mother went to the housing authorities to get help in finding a place of our own. After nearly a week she got a place for the four of us and at the sight of the domicile it was reconfirmed that the severe housing shortage was not a rumor, but a very serious condition that plagued Goerlitz and many other cities. We were actually assigned one single room, about ten feet wide by fifteen feet long, on the first floor of a five-story building, and directly above the laundry or wash room. The only good feature about this place was the tall window straight ahead from the entrance door that looked out to the back yard. To the right side of the window was a bunk bed, Karl-Heinz and I were to sleep on the top and Mother on the bottom. Butting against the foot end of the bunk was a white metal crib for Lothar that looked like it came straight out of an institution. On the other side, against the wall, was a black leatherette bench with backrest and an approximate four-inch slash on the seat that grew longer as the months went by. It seated two, in our case us three kids. The kitchen table and one chair completed the dining area of the room. A two burner cook top and a very tall ceramic tiled oven for our heating needs completed this little home. A toilet and wash basin with running cold water only, was out in the hallway, right next to the door leading into the backyard. I suppose we had to be glad for any kind of shelter, because on the way there we saw families housed in former stores with the big store front window painted over in white for privacy, yet letting daylight in. After the end of WWII, in May of 1945 in Germany, many refugees had returned to the city and gotten apartments according to the number of members in their family. By the time we got back it was either February or March of 1947, and to make matters worse, the occupying Russian military members of rank enjoyed the best and largest apartments. The highest-ranking Russian officers had brought their families to East Germany and lived in villa's, once owned by well to do business men. It became painfully clear to the adults that the east-west border was going to stay, and East Germany was now under the communist rule. To make matters worse the "East", as it became known, was now looked at as a completely different country, and separated from the west. Another drastic change to our city was designating the river, separating the eastern and western part of the city, as the official border between Poland and East Germany. The polish army had taken an entire state, former Silesia (Schlesien), as war restitution and ordered the Germans who remained to leave the new polish territory or be shot. This had made the housing situation about as bad as it could get. All these new rules and borders were already in place before our return to Goerlitz and was obviously not known to Mother. Oma was never interested in politics or borders and most likely did not think these facts were of any consequences or concerns, when Mother decided we were returning back to our home city. While standing near the river and looking across to a part of Germany that became Poland while we lived in Bavaria. No one was allowed too close to the river, and a sign urged to take photos was not permitted. I could see the house where we once lived before evacuating. The roof of the house was gone and all the windows missing, no doubt a result of blowing up the once impressive steel bridge I used to play on, which now rested all broken and twisted in the river. A very sad sight to be sure. Over the ensuing years I would watch a skinny birch tree emerge from the center of the house, but never saw a single person walking, or actually take possession or appeared to be living in any of the empty buildings. It did not seem fair that all the buildings were not lived in, while we barely could keep out of each other's way in our tight quarters.

It was high time to get Karl-Heinz and me back into school, after all, we had missed out over several years. I was assigned to second grade and still remember my teacher's name. Mr. Pannwitz was a most patient and kind man, who no doubt was informed of my recent life and complete freedom in the wild country side of lower Bavaria. I still pity poor Mr. Pannwitz for putting up with my antics, such as going to the bathroom without asking permission or eating a piece of bread when I felt hungry before the recess bell sounded. He tried his best to teach the class that the new regime, namely communism, was a good system to live with. Somehow, I felt his heart was not in what he was forced to teach. It was already March by the time I started classes and remained at that grade level until summer vacation. As luck would have it, my paternal Grandparents wanted me to visit with them near Hamburg, a city in West Germany. I was delighted about that. Another startling fact emerged with great urgency. While some stores were transformed into hopefully temporary housing, most of the remaining stores were completely devoid of any merchandise, be it the dairy store or the butcher shop, the green grocer or the bakery. An emergency kind of soup kitchen was set up at a corner not too far from where we lived, and Mother send either my brother or me with a half-gallon sized container to get the soup of the day. It was usually a nettle soup, a weed that grew everywhere, the kind that stings when it touches the skin, but was edible after it got cooked. There was one fact we found out very quickly, never be amongst the first few in line nor the last few. The large kettle did not get stirred very often, nor did the ingredients get washed too thoroughly, therefore if you were in the beginning of the line you could count on finding some bugs or similar unwanted protein in the soup. On the other hand, if you were amongst the last few in line you would dcfinitcly find a small amount of some sand or soil, including a few pebbles, at the bottom of your plate. One thing was for certain, you would never be a finicky eater for the rest of your life. After just a few days the buggy soup, as we called it, was no longer available, the nearby parks were devoid of any vegetation that could possibly be cooked and pass for food, even many trees were partially stripped of its bark. Somehow mother found out that families who were back in the city by last fall actually received one hundred and ten pounds of potatoes that had to last them all through the winter. At this point I became an asset to our family and had to earn my keep by going from house to house, and from apartment to apartment, to ask the person who opened the door if they could spare some potato peels. We knew there would not be any whole potatoes offered and we had to be grateful for the peelings. I felt embarrassed and depressed knocking on doors and ringing all those bells, is this what I am now, a beggar? After washing the peels several times mother chopped them real small and made potato pancakes, that had a slightly bitter taste, and I hoped never to experience any of that, if I grew up. The thought "if I grew up" was often on my mind, I was never quite sure that I would make it to adulthood, because of the way mother would fly into rages without warning. It became pressing for mother to get a job. She was presentable enough to be hired as a maid for a Russian family, who lived in a villa in walking distance. This job was rather short lived, because mother got overly vocal when she saw their five-year-old son play with flour in a bowl, which he stirred with a hammer. I suppose it was rather unnerving to know we were having little or no food, while this child played with the main ingredient for bread, as if he were in a sand box. He even went after her with the hammer, surely, he sensed she was not fond of children.

The next job location was approximately seventy-five miles away in a mountainous area at a coal mine. I suppose she wondered what to do with the three kids? As luck would have it, she found and re-established the connection with Mommy Deen, who was willing to take care of all three of us. Karl-Heinz and I were overjoyed, but to Lothar she was a stranger and not in the least happy as mother left to work in the coal mine. It was a most difficult time in East Germany, when women had to take jobs that were formerly only held by men. It was very obvious there was an absence of men, especially in mother's age group. The few I did see around the city were not whole in body or mind, they were missing arms or legs. It was not at all unusual to see a man riding a bicycle without any arms, just a leather strap around his neck with the ends of the strap attached to the handlebars and then steering by shifting his shoulders. I really admired their will to try as much as possible to lead a somewhat normal or productive life. One had to wonder about what could be considered normal in such times. After seeing a man without legs, who pushed himself forward with the knuckles of his hands while perched on a three-by-three foot piece of wood, to which some unmatched wheels had been attached. I came to realize the man without arms was more fortunate, he still got around fast. The man without legs had no chance to obtain a wheelchair, and without prosthetics even homemade crutches would be useless. After mother left for work at the coal mines life with Mommy Deen was not in the least bit better, as far as getting food was concerned. She worried constantly about providing nutrition for a clan of five. Besides the three of us she also cared for a seven-year-old girl, whose mother was not interested to raise her own child. The reason became obvious after just a few days. That girl was an ill-tempered and sneaky little witch, but Mommy Deen said to overlook her behavior because she was just unhappy. What a wonderful and compassionate woman I thought and wished with all my heart to live with her forever. The devaluation of money did not help in her quest to buy a loaf of bread. She would leave in the morning with just about a rucksack full of paper money and hike out of the city in hopes to get a bread from a farmer, who would be willing to accept all that paper money for the bread. Sometimes she would not get back until late afternoon or evening, by then it was time to think about dinner. On those days it was my job to peel about three potatoes, which she would then grate and add to a rather large pot of boiling water. A little salt and some onions completed that feast after it boiled for about twenty minutes. She called this a Zudelsuppe, it sounded like a funny word and I had no idea where that word came from, but it suited this soup just fine. After a little more than a week living with Mommy Deen, she had to get in touch with Mother, because Lothar was not eating and did a lot of crying. We supposed he missed his mother and were afraid he would get seriously ill. Mother appeared the following week end and took her youngest offspring with her. Much later we found out how she coped with a three-and-a-half-year-old at a time and place where the idea of a babysitter was not an option. She simply took him with her to the mine she was working at, spread a blanket under a tree and tied a piece of a clothes line around his middle and the other end to the tree, giving him just enough slack to move around on the blanket. A few objects acting as toys kept him busy until her lunch break, which she spend with him. While he was taking his nap, she would return to the mine to work underground until the end of her shift. It became a little more challenging on the days it rained, when a borrowed umbrella did the trick to keep him mostly dry. I am sure this was a very difficult time for her, but I was just happy to be with Mommy Deen. It became increasingly more challenging to keep the little guy on the blanket all day. He got bored and became more difficult by the day. The weather was not helping any either and mother needed to find another job back home. Her next employment was with the rail road working on a demolition crew. Her job was to remove railroad ties from defunct tracks to be reused elsewhere. This was hard work for sure, but I never heard her complain. She did mention that working outside was an improvement over the coal mine.

After summer vacation time was over the normal routine of going to school got started. I had finished second grade and entered third grade but was still two years behind. To my benefit I looked younger than my ten years and being small of stature worked for me too. I started third grade and found the going pretty easy. Our classes started at eight in the morning until four in the afternoon from Monday through Friday, with five minutes between classes and half an hour for lunch. On Saturday's we only had class from eight until noon time but got more homework than during the week. The reason for that was having one and a half days to do it, no complaints, that was the accepted rule. After about six weeks of third grade, I received the most awesome news: I was being transferred to the fourth grade, but on a trial basis only. If I was not able to catch up and stay on track my return to the previous level was assured. This was the greatest news for me at that point, because I always felt I was smart enough in spite of Mother calling me a dumb cow or a stupid goat whenever she was on a rant. I used to feel terribly hurt after her outbursts, especially after people had complimented me about my having big, beautiful and friendly eyes and they suspected I was smart as well. It was my sincerest desire not to be sent back to third grade class, I was going to make sure of that by applying myself to the work ahead of me. Now I was only one year behind age wise, but strangely enough this did not bother me at all any more. It was apparent to me that this information was not made public in class, so I found it comforting that the kids in class accepted me as one of them. Even at this early age I had but one goal in my mind. I knew that I would not stay one day past my eighteenth birthday with her. The moment I was done with school I would just disappear. At eighteen I would be of age and no urging of Mothers would move the police to come looking for me and dragging me back home. In the meantime, I enjoyed the time with Mommy Deen. Then something unspeakable caught my eye on the report card. Among all the "A's" and "B's" I spotted a big fat "D" in geography. Not acceptable to me. I was going to fix that in short time. Sure enough, by next grading time I had earned an A. This made me feel smarter and satisfied with the result of just a little bit of extra time spent on studies.

One day I discovered an infected splinter, or whatever this was, on the palm of my right hand. Over the next few days, I watched a most interesting thin red line just under the skin, that seemed to climb from the palm of my hand past the wrist and then up the arm. As the line reached just above the elbow bend of the arm, I decided to show Mommy Deen this strange occurrence. She was immediately alarmed and send me at once to the local clinic to have it checked. There was some talk about blood poisoning between a doctor and a nurse, but all I was interested in was the wonderfully impressive looking brace that now adorned my right arm as I left the clinic. The brace kept my arm bent at the elbow and reached from just a few inches above the elbow to the beginning of my fingers. I was instructed to keep the brace on for a couple weeks and saw immediately the benefit of this ever so delightful dilemma. It simply meant no homework for the duration. The kids in my class gave the brace their stamp of approval and envied me for not having to write the homework assignments down. Of course, I did keep up with the class, just not by writing.

As usually, when everything seemed to go so well, there was a change about to happen. Our time with Mommy Deen came to an end and we were back at the one room living quarters. Most likely it was about the unusual circumstances that had forced mother to take a small child to work, namely the coal mines. As the weather turned colder this routine became unacceptable and so ended her job. A few kids on the block and I discovered that a truck loaded with coal or briquette would be driven along our street every now and then, so naturally the two oldest boys would jump on the back of the truck and toss as many briquettes as possible onto the street. The rest of us would gather this treasure and then divide it amongst us kids, because coal for the winter was also rationed, just like potatoes. I'm not sure if the driver was aware of this, or if he just felt sorry for the poor horde running in the street, but this certainly helped every one of us to augment the allotted amount of coal for the winter. It was common for children to wear long, brown cotton stockings in the winter that were attached to an undergarment that almost defied description. If really pressed to explain, I would say it may resemble an about ten-inch-wide bra with buttons in the back, but without cups. It had an elastic strap attached to each side to connect with the button on the outside top of the stocking and was worn by girls and boys alike. These stockings had to be washed once a week, this would always be done Saturday afternoon, because we only had half a day of school. Karl-Heinz's and my stockings would then be hung on a makeshift line or draped over the back of a chair next to the tall, tiled oven to dry. Most of the time this would suffice, but I do remember one particular Monday morning when I found the stockings had not completely dried. I put them on in the damp condition and left for school on that wintery day. I am not sure how long after that day I felt excruciating pain in both of my knees, so much so, that I could not bend either leg to get up the two steps in front of the house. I leaned first to one side to maneuver the first step with a stiffened leg and then did the same tilt on the other side. Since I don't remember any more about that painful condition, I guess it did not last very long, but I was just a little worried that I might have rheumatism, a condition I had heard about from mother's aunt Clara, in connection with old age. No worries about that yet. Poor Aunt Clara had many aches, pains and even sciatica. She always walked with a slight tilt forward and had to wear a strong brace. She was nice enough, and I was lucky to be able to stay with her for about a week at her very lovely apartment, when I suffered from whooping cough. This, I was sure, was meant to protect my two brothers from catching the same illness. Trying to sleep in an almost sitting position was very difficult and the constant coughing was extremely painful. I abstained from breathing deeply and took only shallow breaths to avoid some of the pain. It felt like my ribs got bruised from all that coughing. While staying at Aunt Clara's apartment I discovered that she had a wonderful looking piano. I was aching to touch it, but I was still too sick. She told me that after I got just a little older, I may come and play. I did take her up on that promise way too soon after my recovery, but her nerves were not up to my pinging away at the keyboard.

 After getting back to our tight quarters I tried hard to be inconspicuous at home, I even avoided looking directly at mothers face because of the often made remark "why are you looking at me so stupid". I always thought people could act stupid, but not look stupid, yet somehow, she must have mastered the art of detecting stupidity just by looking at someone. This, I believe, may have been the point in my life when l really started to dislike her, maybe even hate her just a little at times. This feeling was re-enforced after she got a hold of a whip called a cat and nine tails. It had a wood handle from which hung nine thin strips of leather, about fifteen or eighteen inches long. I swore there were more than nine strips on that fat handle, and she had a sound explanation for acquiring this new weapon: she wanted to avoid hurting her hands on our hard heads. Karl-Heinz and I were really scared of her now, especially since she made us bring the whip to her from its place between the tiled oven and the wall. This felt like an announcement of what was to come, but Lothar escaped that kind of punishment, because of his age, I assumed. The next time we were beaten with the whip brother, and I decided to make a pact. We were going to eliminate one of the leather strips after each whipping, hoping fewer strips would hurt less. When alone at home, we lit one of the gas burners and held one strip over the flame until burnt through, but this took far too long. We had to find a better way, and we did. As luck would have it we got a hold of a razor blade, from then on after every punishment we cut one strip off. Either she did not notice it or care, but after several months there was only one strip left and we experienced firsthand that fewer strips did not hurt less. That thing hissed as it cut through the air and stung our backs, and with the last one gone the only thing left was the wood handle, that was flung in our direction and never seen again. From then on anything within her reach was a weapon, from wooden spoons to clothes hangers and more. Having learned from experience I became very adept at protecting my face, and at the slightest sudden motion from Mother, my hands would fly up and cross at the wrist in anticipation and for protection. This did not help one day while at home with a cold. I was resting on the upper bunk and the little guy was just finished with his nap. To entertain him I devised a game of "wolves are going to get you." Whenever I said that phrase, he would raise his hands and I hoisted him from his crib to the upper bunk. He giggled with such delight as I repeated that motion a few more times. This activity must have shifted the wooden slats holding the mattress in place. At the precise moment I intended to lift my brother up again, the door flew open, I fell between the slats to the bottom bunk, and Mother reached the bunks in two flying leaps, all while she yanked the scarf off her head and started to hit me with her head scarf. The shock of the bed collapsing and the sudden appearance of Mother on the scene gave me such a fright that I passed out cold. She may have inadvertently mentioned my fainting to her Mom, my Oma, as well as Mothers sister Frieda, who has always lived with Oma. The ladies advised Mother to take me to a heart specialist, because someone my age should not be fainting that easily. The appointment was established, and the lady doctor took me into her examining room. Several questions and a quick exam later, the doctor gave Mother her expert diagnosis: a murmur of the heart due to emotional influences. This did not sit right with Mother at all, she called the doctor a quack, grabbed me by the hand and yanked me out of the office. That was the last official examination I had received by a licensed doctor for some time to come.

Mother was at work and school was out, therefore I wanted to pay a quick visit to Mommy Deen. On the way there I passed a now defunct former textile factory. It was an imposing brick corner building with large windows at street level that had iron bars on the outside. Were those bars to keep someone out, or were they to keep people in? It did look a lot like I imagined a prison might look. In passing I glanced at a window sill and discovered a shiny object just inside the bars. Interesting, I thought, as I stopped to pick up the item of interest and discovered it was a key. It looked new and was very light in weight, not like our ancient house key, or even Oma's older than old and heavy, five- or six-inches long key that could have unlocked a big castle door. I looked around, not sure for what, but I took the interesting thing with me to be tried out on any door I would come across. I showed it to Mommy Deen, who told me this key was made of aluminum, that's why it did not weigh as much as a regular key. After I got back home, I tried the key on the large house door, but it was way too short, not a fit at all. Next, I tried it at the door to our miniscule world. It slid into the lock easily and my heart started to race, as I slowly turned the key, thereby locking and unlocking the door repeatedly. I could hardly believe that this light weight thing would open our room door and could not wait to tell Karl-Heinz about this amazing find. What were we going to do after we opened that door? There was not much we could do, since that key only opened our interior door, but we were somehow going to make use of it. One thing was for sure: this was our secret, not to be divulged to anyone. Mother was working the late shift from four p.m. until one a.m. this entire month, so we could enjoy partial freedom from being locked up in our tiny world. We waited until Lothar was asleep, then unlocked our door and stood in the hallway of this four-story building, not knowing what to do about this newfound mini freedom, because the main door as well as the door to the backyard were locked for the night. As if we shared the same brain waves, we took our two footstools into the hallway, positioning them next to the closed door, then we sat down and started to sing old German folk songs in harmony. Both of us loved music, but our old radio was forever broken, no matter how many times we spliced or twisted its wires. I am sure we gave it the final death fix. It appears the neighbors on the first couple floors in earshot appreciated our singing. Some actually came out of their apartments, listened for a while and gave us some change. Karl-Heinz and I were very pleased with this unexpected windfall and we hoped we would get enough money to experience what it felt like to be rich. Our idea of being rich was very modest, plus we knew the neighbors liked our singing. This activity went on for a few more evenings, we gladly accepted the money, but then it came to a halt, because mothers work schedule had changed once again. Our musical career was over, and one day mother mentioned as matter of fact that she was told by some neighbors they had heard us singing and thought we sounded very nice. Our mother never ever did hear us sing and I really felt it was her misfortune. I wonder whatever happen to that shiny key, it was of no use to us anymore.

My attention was diverted to a new and very worrisome dilemma. I noticed many dime and nickel sized infected spots up and down my legs. Mother was not able to identify the spots and send me off to the clinic. After cleaning out the puss the spots looked like rather deep holes, were filled with some kind of salve and wrapped with a bandage of questionable material. It certainly was not gauze, but I caught snippets of the conversation between the doctor and the nurse, that had me worried. To heck with the non-gauze wrapping, the word pox stuck in my mind, and I immediately thought of smallpox. Oh, my goodness, these pox are going to spread to my face and I will be disfigured forever. The nurse assured me these were not that kind of pox, and I released a long sigh of relief. On my walk home I had to make numerous stops to rewind the bandages that stretched from the upper thighs to just above the ankles. The bandage material felt exactly like crepe paper and would loosen after every few steps and just slide down. I barely walked about a block when it became necessary to rewrap each leg from top to bottom. It took quite a while to get home that afternoon.

Perseverance paid off for mother, and we finally got a bigger place to live, along with a new job for her at a factory that produced brick making machinery and steam engines on a large scale. Mother's new job was as a drill press operator doing piece work, working a different shift every month. The new apartment, if you could call two rooms an apartment for four people, was on the top floor of a five-story walkup. The toilet and only source of water, and cold at that, was located on the landing between the fourth and fifth floors. We now had a rather large room that served as a bedroom for mother and living room in one, and there was a separate kitchen with a rather small dormered window on a slanted wall, not much bigger than the usual bathroom window. It sure looked like a long way down to the cobble stoned back yard but looking out of the kitchen window I discovered the roof of the landing was within reach. If I could somehow get onto that roof from the little window, there were possibilities of all kinds to use that space. There was an impressive view of all the nearby roof tops and a church steeple from the kitchen as well as the big room, which had a large window that let enough light in to make the room look bright and friendly. After living at this new address for only about a month I had an idea how to use the roof over the stairway landing.

I was able to crouch on the small window sill of the kitchen, reach out to the rain gutter and swing one leg over it. The rest was easy enough with sufficient upper body strength, and once I stood on the tar papered surface, I felt like I was on top of the world. Eventually I got a hold of a shoe box in which I transported soil to my roof garden to be. I was very proud of all that work, and since the ground floor housed a store that sold seeds and things a real gardener might use, I had a source to get some items from the son of the store owner. My garden to be consisted of one row of soil about five feet long and one foot wide, but only about four or five inches deep. After planting some beans that were supposed to grow into string beans, as well as some carrot seeds, I watered all every day. Sure enough, soon little green stems and tiny leaves appeared, and the bean stalks started to climb up the slanted roof. At this time Mother had a boyfriend we called Uncle Helmut, who was kid friendly and a great guy. Whenever he came to visit, I liked him more and more and hoped Mother would marry him. He worked for the railroad and obviously made enough money and never forgot to bring brother and me a small bag of candy. One day, as he entered the kitchen, he saw my leg disappear out the window and was horrified when he saw me on the roof. I explained what was going on, but I had to promise to immediately stop this activity, or he would tell Mother all about these dangerous acrobatics. The beanstalks were already about five feet tall, and the carrot tops were getting full and bushy. I did make the promise to him, but first I pulled on a carrot top to see if anything was happening below in the soil. To my big surprise there was an actual orange looking carrot in the shape of an L. I guess they could have used a few more inches of soil to grow straight. Things did not go very smoothly in class either. The boy sitting behind me was constantly pulling on my braids, thus making my head jerk to one side or the other. Thinking that ignoring this would finally make him stop did not work at all, even a warning of consequences from me just made him laugh. As soon as the bell rang and our teacher left the class room I turned and smacked him hard in the face, ignoring the fact he wore glasses. To my surprise he reciprocated with a punch to my midsection, this meant war. In our school the hallways were never clogged with students, instead the teachers moved from one class room to the next, except when a rare fight broke out. Our altercation did not stay in the class room but spilled out into the hallway with the whole class forming an ever moving circle around us. While punches were flying with me sometimes on top of him and just seconds later him on top of me, I was surprised to hear the boys cheering me on, all the while the girls were cheering for him. There was no time to analyze the reason for this, for suddenly I felt being lifted by the back of my coat to the upright position, as was my adversary. Wright or wrong was quickly sorted out or dismissed, but the boy's mother had to come to school at the end of classes. She took me to her home where she exchanged my coat with one of hers, so mine could be cleaned after rolling on the dirty floor. It was winter, the school presumably ran out of coal, so classes were held with us wearing our coats and gloves.

There were other tenants on our floor and we shared a long corridor. On our side, but facing the street, lived two old ladies and one old gentleman, whom Karl-Heinz and I immediately called Opa, an endearing name for Grandpa. I have no idea what the relationship between these lovely people was and did not care, but we spent many an evening in their company when mother worked the late or night shift. We would play cards or just talk. At the other end of the hallway lived a married couple who had no children, of whom we knew nothing and did not interact with. The three seniors shared a big room as their living room and kitchen, it also served as the bedroom for the two ladies. Opa had a smaller bedroom all to himself, with an entrance off the big room and an additional door to the hallway. He was a rather frail person and I worried if he got enough to eat. One evening, while Mother was at work, our card game ran right into their last meal of the day. Karl-Heinz and I were invited to eat with them, but we knew the limited food supply could make this a hardship for these very nice neighbors. We declined in a friendly way but stayed around just long enough to observe the preparation of Opa's meal that evening. My heart went out to him as I watched him pour some salt on a little four by eight-inch wood cutting board, then proceeded to grind the salt with a flat knife until it turned into a fine powder. Next, he spread it on a dry slice of rye bread but added a few sprinkles of water I assume to make it easier to swallow. This and a cup of tea was his dinner. I left their room in a hurry, because I did not want them to see the tears that flooded my eyes. We were all quite poor at this point, but my little family had at least some margarine to spread on our bread. By now we had ration cards that did anyone little good. What use is a meat ration when no meat was available at the butcher shop? Instead, you could get one egg for 125 grams of meat ration, which mother would turn into scrambled eggs for us by stretching that egg with flour and water. On the rare occasion when the butcher shop had meat available there was never a selection. Everyone had to be content with what was offered, either chopped meat or bits of stew meat. When Mother was able to make stew us kids would have three or four small bite sized pieces of meat along with potatoes and carrots. One Christmas holiday she actually was able to get four smoked chubs, a kind of herring, one for each of us. We were in a festive mood and really enjoyed our dinner. Unfortunately, during the night all four of us got very sick, and we hurled that dinner as if it was just on loan to our bodies, or as if it was poison. Our bodies were not used to so much fat or oil and could not accept it. Word on the street circulated that eating yeast will make you feel less hungry, even full and satisfied. We were able to purchase some at the nearby bakery with the excuse our mother was going to bake a cake for some invented occasion or other. As overheard by other kids I placed a thin slice of yeast onto a saucer and sprinkled just a little of Mother's precious sugar over the top that started a melting action almost instantly. It was best to eat this before it was completely melted and the sugar did help to camouflage the not so pleasant taste of the yeast. This activity was stopped as fast as it had started, because of the death of a seventeen-year-old boy, who had consumed a dangerous amount of yeast. Apparently, it expanded in his stomach, as it is supposed to in order to give you that being full and sated feeling, as well as in the intestines, to such a degree that a tear in the intestines caused his death. In order to drive that point into every young brain it was mandatory for most classes to attend the funeral. After that occurrence I literally stooped to a new low to ward off hunger. I am very embarrassed to admit to picking up discarded apple cores, brush off any hint of dirt and finishing them off right down to the stem and seeds. This awful activity was noticed by Karl-Heinz, but he never mentioned that disgusting habit to me or our mother. I had wondered, but never asked him, as to what he did in order not to be very concerned about going hungry. It was many years into adulthood when he gave up this childhood secret. He actually had befriended a classmate whose father owned, or was in charge of, a butcher shop and the two boys would go there after school and get a few slices of bologna. I felt just a little retroactive anger over his selfish acts, but also understood why he had to keep that secret. As soon as word got around that a certain store had something, in fact anything eatable for sale, long lines were forming in an instant, with people standing three deep and stretching up to three blocks long. Half way through the line they usually ran out of whatever was offered and people walked away dejectedly, hoping for better luck next time. It was not unusual for people forming lines before they even knew what was for sale at the store, as long as you had a place in line was more important. Then someone would go to find out what was to be had that day.

    I never thought it strange at all, in fact we never even wondered, why we never saw a dog being walked on the streets, or on the loose. How could anyone keep a pet when there was hardly any food for people? I know for a fact that I have eaten horse meat and liked it. Mother's girlfriend Kate had a lung disease and received a ration card for horse meat. There was also no doubt in my mind that at least on one occasion we had some dog meat in our stew, Mother never denied it, she just smiled. Ration cards had been issued to every family according to how many people were in that family. As long as my youngest brother lived with us, we received four cards that covered every item of food, from meat to bread, from butter to sugar. There was also a ration for milk on the same card, but only children under the age of nine were eligible to have whole milk, the rest of us had to get skimmed milk, which Mother used in her fake coffee or to make flour soup or oatmeal for breakfast. Oh, how I hated that oatmeal soup, because it contained many pieces of its shell that scratched when you ate it and would scratch again as they left at the other end. I would push those bits with my spoon onto the rim of the soup plate, at which time Mother would give me a slap at the back of my head while yelling to stop picking and just eat. Whenever mother sent me to the dairy store to get whole milk, I could never curb my urgent need to sneak a couple sips. After returning with that precious liquid, usually by the third floor, I would lift the white enameled container to my lips and gulp just one or two sips with the greatest of enjoyment, then race to the last landing before our floor to the water spigot. I looked around to make sure I was not observed while I filled the container just to the one-liter line. After handing mother the milk I was prepared for her outburst of "those bastards are messing with the milk again", because after just one look she could determine with undeniable certainty, that water had been added by the telltale, but ever so slight blue hue of the liquid. I was just hoping she would not have enough courage, or anger, to storm into the dairy store and make that accusation. Most women were somewhat happy with what was available without making a big fuss, in fear they might be cut off or blackballed by overly zealous neighbors with aspiration to make a good name for themselves with the communist party. One thing was for sure, the communist party ruled and nothing was done without their sanction.

With our small apartment came a storage space in the cellar of the building, used for storing seasonal items, most of all coal for heating in the winter months. Then there was the allotted one hundred metric pounds of potatoes delivered in late fall, that had to last until the early crop the following summer. It was either Karl-Heinz's or my job to go into the cellar to bring enough of either in a bucket up to the fifth floor, but mostly it was my job. Getting anything from the cellar was not my favorite chore, because the place was cold, dark and drafty, but mostly dark. There was no light, therefore I had to take a candle and matches along with the usual bucket. As I stood by the cellar door contemplating my journey into the depth of darkness, I had to admit a certain amount of fear gripped my imagination. In my mind there was no place without some living things, either good or bad, that is why a cellar had to have bad and ferocious animals in its depth. I knew there had to be wild beasts and snarling dragons, all of whom could smell fear oozing out of my pores and think of me as easy prey. I told myself to be confident, not a scared and silly human, but instead let the beasts know I was coming in peace and not afraid. Next, I let them know I was not going to hurt them, as they might be afraid of me as well. The plan was to whistle a nice tune, to signal I was a good human and wished no harm. Now it was time to light the candle, but just as I opened the door the strong draft blew it out at once, undoubtedly blown from a dragon's mouth. After relighting the candle, I gathered my last bit of courage and made my way down the stairs, whistling all the while, walking quickly to our storage cubicle, while trying not to appear scared out of my mind. I must admit the most frightening part was getting potatoes from the dungeon that is what I called the cellar. In winter they grow white sprouts that get thicker and longer by the week, until they resemble menacing white snakes. Of course, I whistled and hummed every time I left the dungeon, trying not to run up the stairs in a complete panic, but walking tall and with confidence as if I was in total control of the situation and my somewhat fragile emotions. There was another reason to go to the cellar every Saturday evening that was in preparation for our weekly bath. It was Karl-Heinz's and my job to get our approximately five feet long bathtub up to our apartment. This tub was made of light weight zinc metal, light enough for brother and me to carry, holding it upside down like a canoe over our heads, up the five floors. Not an easy task for sure, but a necessity, since the fifth floor as housing for families was most likely an afterthought and not originally laid out with bathroom facilities in mind. The monthly rent reflected the lack of available convenience, there was no extra pay for the view. The challenge getting the tub up all the way was the fact that the light was on a timer that would turn off every twenty or so seconds. We were fleet footed, but this was ridiculous. We barely made it up two floors when the light went off and one of us had to grope in the dark for the button to turn on the light again. In the meantime, Mother had already her largest pot full of water on the cast iron portion of the tiled stove. As soon as the water neared the boiling point it was poured into the zinc tub with an almost equal amount of cold water added, now the bath was ready for the first two bodies. To prepare a bath for four people individually was just too labor intensive for mother, therefore the rule was two to a tub. I was lucky to choose first as the eldest, so with my scientific reasoning I chose littlest brother Lothar: small body, less dirt on him, but of course he got to go before me. Naturally I was not thrilled stepping into a previously used tub of water, but after I scrubbed clean, I got to stand up and get rinsed off with a pitcher of clean warm water. Now the tub had to be emptied, the bathtub ring removed and cleaned properly, then the whole procedure was repeated so first Karl-Heinz and then Mother could have their bath. The same routine was performed every Saturday evening, no matter what. Another thing I did not like about bath time was the fact that I had to scrub Mothers back. To see her seated naked in that tub every Saturday was not something I looked forward to. She was not at all embarrassed about her nakedness in front of me, so where did my dislike to see her that way come from? Another reason were her rather numerous stretch marks on her abdomen and breasts, they definitely were my fault, because they appeared while she was pregnant with me and got worse with my two brothers. All I can say is that karma must be a female named bitch, because I inherited the same type of skin with limited elasticity that gave me plenty of stretch marks under the same circumstances.

Insert: one day when gym

One late afternoon the two old ladies knocked on our kitchen door while Mother was at work and urged me to come quickly to Opa's room. There were two doors to enter his room, one from the hall way and one from their large room. The hallway door was always locked, so I had to follow through their big room into his. One look at him told me that he was very ill. His face appeared quite sunken in and the grey stubble covering his lower face made his chin look even pointier. His already frail body looked even more so, even while somewhat concealed under the skimpy cover. I sat at the edge of his bed and held his hand, while he managed to give me a hint of a smile. It seemed to me like he wanted to say good bye, but I was not willing to accept that notion at this or any time. Speaking to him softly about everything that happened on that day, and nothing, I kept on holding his bony hand. It seemed I had sat there for quite a while when I noticed his hand was feeling colder than when I first held it. One of the ladies touched my shoulder and whispered that he was gone. The feeling of severe loss of such a kind person gave me a kind of pain I had never felt before. Having seen bodies in the past was sad for sure, but they were strangers who never entered my life before. I have never forgotten this kind old man, even though I never knew his given name. To me he was simply Opa and I missed him for a very long time.

Not long after his death we were allowed to use that room, and after a quick paint job it became mine and Karl-Heinz's bedroom. To my surprise Mother got us new beds, the head and foot boards were in glossy white, the mattress for each bed came in three pieces, and I guess this configuration was for easy transporting in case of moving to another apartment. One of the first things I did was to flip the sheets and cover towards the foot end, then remove the middle section of the mattress. This exposed two of the boards so I could sit on one and draw a piano keyboard in pencil on the other board that held the mattress in place. It was a job well done and to me it looked like a real piano. I dare say that I gave the most astounding silent performances on my "piano". The classics have never sounded better and the imaginary audience rewarded me with thunderous applause and shouts of "bravo". Even though Karl-Heinz and I shared the room he never knew or saw my "piano." He and I thought it was real nice of our mother to get us new beds, so we wanted to do something nice in return. Every time she sends one of us to get some grocery item we would snip a tiny piece of twenty-five grams of sugar ration from the card, until we had two hundred and fifty grams accumulated to buy her a nice little box of fondant candy in time for mother's day. We had also collected a few pennies from the change at each purchase. This was to be our very first ever present to her and we looked forward to the presentation. Unfortunately, she never received her candy, as another beating nullified our intent. Instead, we decided we deserved to get a candy each in the shape of a teddy bear that was the same amount of sugar ration. We were licking at the sweet treasure with such enthusiasm while walking along Main Street, completely engrossed and ignoring of the fact that we walked into the street at a red light. As luck would have it, we walked right into the belly of a policeman, who I swore could tell our sweet treat was an ill-gotten gain. We just stuttered our apologies after his short reprimand and went on our way with a slightly urgent step. But I managed to mar my new headboard real soon, due to my love of reading. Mother had removed the light bulb from our room to stop us from staying up too late and running up the electric bill. I had an old flashlight, but no batteries, so I was forced to confiscate candles from the Christmas tree in order to read the most fabulous thin books my dearest girlfriend Helga L. lend me. Those skinny books were all about America and Tom Mix, the greatest Indian fighter in all that country. His adventures were my escape from my life. I knew someday I would be in America and fight Indians, just like Tom Mix, therefore I would practice pretending to be asleep next to the camp fire, all the while peering through half closed eye lids in anticipation of approaching savages. Thirteen-year-olds are so impressionable. Helga had stacks of those books and lend them to me without reservation, but occasionally I would fall asleep while the candle was burning down completely, and at one point left a deep charred mark on the very white headboard. I was lucky the smell of smoke woke me from sleep and avoided a major catastrophe. My brother, being clueless as always, never noticed a thing and slept through it all. I worked real hard at sandpapering that deeply charred spot out of the headboard, then fill in the cleaned dent with putty and paint it white with nail polish from dear Helga. Then give it that glossy look with clear nail polish. After that scary incident I stopped reading for a while, because I knew I could not entirely trust myself not to fall asleep and burn the whole house down to the ground. I could have never done any of that cover up without the help of my dear friend Helga and I'm sure her mom's input. Her family was in a similar situation as mine, with the difference my father was dead, while hers was in prison. He was caught smuggling some goods from West to East Germany to make life a little better for his family but got caught by the authorities and received an eight year prison term, I never met the man. Her mom was a very kind lady who always made me feel welcome, but Mother would never allow me to have my friend over, even when I explained we would like to do our homework together. Her reaction was "are you so stupid you can't do your homework on your own?" Helga L. was as sweet as her mom and proved it on several occasions. One of these was a parent teacher meeting at school on a Saturday, which Mother could not attend because she had to work. We were asked to bring a plate along as there was going to be some food served. The excitement was great as I slid down the banister as usual, but that excitement turned to instant panic when I dropped the plate. Of course, it shattered into many pieces and I ran to Helga's apartment in tears explaining the mishap. Her Mom calmed me down and gave me one of her plates to keep. Mother would never have noticed a different plate, as we did not have a matching set anyway. Another time our class was going on a planned class trip in the country side, for which I had no clothes to wear. Yet once again Helga's Mom came to the rescue by lending me a pair of shorts and a top, and I have a picture to prove it. On one occasion, while walking home from school, Helga let me wear her pretty soft leather shoes with a cushiony rubber sole, obviously one of the successfully smuggled in items from the west, for about five minutes. Because I had a slightly bigger foot than hers, it was my decision not to wear them longer than five minutes, because I did not want to ruin her pretty shoes. Mine were of regular leather that in itself was an enormous step up from the previous year's sandals made of a plastic called Igelit that I wore summer and the first part of that winter. In the summer they were soft and very flexible, but in the winter months the material got quite hard and one or the other strap would break almost regularly. My brother and I got real adept at fixing that by heating a flat knife over a gas flame, then hold it against one end of the strap until it almost melted, then pressing the two ends of the straps together until they fused. The only good thing about these miserable Igelit sandals was the fact that you could cut a piece off the straight edge of the heel and use it as an eraser for eliminating mistakes from in pencil written homework. While taking a break from reading I had the opportunity to trade my pocket knife for a cute white mouse, including two doll house sized dishes, of course she was named Snowflake, and we bonded instantly. She resided in my wardrobe and was played with after returning from school, all unbeknownst to Mother. One day, after I had finished my homework, I decided to give Snowflake some loving attention. While engrossed in play with my pal the door suddenly opened and in just a fraction of a second, I shoved her under my sweater. After the question of "what are you doing" Mother's eyes grew really big, as she watched this strange bump under the sweater move in different directions, to finally exit at my neck. I did not get punished that day but was ordered to get rid of "that mouse." I was now again in possession of my pocket knife.

There was one person in class shorter than me, we shared the same school desk, and for some unknown reason we both decided to squeeze ourselves into the lower cabinet in the physics class room. As luck would have it, that cabinet had the turn off valve for the Bunsen burner. Just seconds after the teacher lit the burner one of us would turn off the valve and the whole class giggled. After doing this once more the teacher became aware of what was going on. The space was so cramped, and we needed to stretch, perhaps even exit the cabinet. No such luck. The teacher had wedged a chair just so to block our exit for the duration of the class, then after dismissing the other students he let us out. The disciplinary action required us to write one hundred and fifty times "I will not disrupt the class". At home I was forced to be timid and quiet, so it was no wonder I got a bit uppity at school. I did not want to waste my limited amount of paper on a "punishment assignment," so I got a really great idea, at least I thought it was rather genius.

Going from apartment to apartment, even in the adjoining buildings, I collected old newspapers and cut the margins off to write my disciplinary assignment, which was also the headline. The teacher's eyes went big when I handed him proudly the bundle of L-shaped paper strips with my work. He took it as being more rebellious and commanded me to write the same sentence two hundred and fifty times. I was also instructed to leave off the headline. I felt crushed but undefeated, collected more newspapers and wrote again as before. I guess he gave up, because he did not even make mention of my headline. The first year and a half of my two-year religious instructions, a wish of Oma's and a requirement in order to have Confirmation, was interesting and even amusing. Pastor Hauser was a total bully towards the boys, but rather easy on the girls. If a boy was unable to recite a verse by heart, he could expect to have his head shoved into the nearest wall. The girls merely got a tongue lashing and then went on with the lecture. We were definitely not of a delicate snowflake generation und never told on the Pastor. He only lived about three blocks away from our apartment building in a single-family home, that had a small fenced in front yard with a not very tall apple tree. The apples looked very inviting though small, we called them paradise apples and were going to have some. One of the boys climbed the tree and filled his pant pockets, while the pastor's housekeeper yelled from the second-floor window. We shared the bounty and were satisfied to have put one over on the mean pastor. After passing the religious tests we were ready for the big day. Mother and I had sporadic communications with my paternal grandparents, mostly by picture postcards. They lived in a very picturesque city near Hamburg in northern West Germany. To write letters was useless because of the strict censorship. Whole lines or sentences would be blocked out with black ink if the content of that sentence mentioned something positive or informative about the West. No letter was exempt from being opened and scrutinized for "objectionable" content. Anyway, my grandparents send a dress and a pair of beautiful shoes, made of black patent leather and suede, to wear at my confirmation. Also included was a chromatic harmonica with song book. Being a music lover since ever and having learned to read notes at school, I played one song after the other. While playing with real gusto I was surprised to hear a rather urgent knocking at my bedroom door. It actually was more like pounding. I knew Mother was at work and she would most certainly not knock, so I opened to find the end-of-the-hall neighbor standing there with an angry look on his face. He lectured me on never to play that particular song, because it was against the law, and he would report me to the authorities if I persisted. He informed me that piece was the national anthem of West Germany and therefore forbidden. Of course, I promised to comply. My confirmation took place on March 30th of 1952. The night before this monumental day was our usual bath ritual, my hair was washed, and Mother started to comb out the tangles. Unbeknownst to me she had secretly motioned Karl-Heinz to get her the scissors. Suddenly I heard a crunching sound just beyond my right ear, and in a flash, I grabbed my hair just before the cut was completed. Rage was rising from inside me but had to contain it fast while she was still holding the scissors. For my confirmation pictures I still wanted to have my braids immortalized, but she obviously had different ideas. I never did have a luxurious head of hair, but now my braids really looked a bit skimpy. Next morning, we awoke to two inches of snow that fell overnight and I hated to walk to church with my new shoes. Mother had actually saved up enough of the ration cards to bake two sheet cakes for the occasion. The party was a huge success and I received cards with money from the relatives, who were Mothers aunts and uncles, plus one of her cousins named Lenchen, who was also my godmother. She gave me a most wonderful black attaché case, also known as a briefcase, that was to serve me in my chosen profession. I was on top of the world as I totaled up the cash later that afternoon. It did not take long for me to decide what to buy, for I had my eyes on a pair of red leather shoes that would use up only half of my money on hand. The other half was to be saved in case of an emergency or a future purchase. After school the next day I went to the shoe store and tried them on. They looked fabulous and I bought them on the spot. Mother liked my shoes too and went on and on about wanting a pair just like mine. This was no idle talk, she said she wants a pair just like that, this was not just a hint either, and she really wanted those shoes. In an effort to keep her still festive mood I gave in to her wish, I got her the shoes and inwardly I called her many not so nice names for being a selfish witch. That trait was frequently displayed at the table during the evening meal. She would cut a rather hefty slice of rye bread for Karl-Heinz and I, not a bad thing, spread some margarine on it and top it off with one slice of bologna, which she would stretch to make sure it covered most of the bread. Her slice was cut quite thin and topped with two or three slices of bologna. Brother had the nerve to reach for another slice of meat, but her hand holding the knife came down on the back of his hand so fast, if I had blinked I would have missed it. About three times per year, we would receive a package from America. The excitement was always great because we knew there would be chewing gum, chocolate and Nestlé's hot chocolate powder, as well as some items of female clothing. Mother usually tried everything on first, if it did not fit her it became mine. I still remember two particular dresses and a bright red winter coat with big black buttons. You could see me coming from a mile away and I was very proud of it. Lothar actually missed out on most of these surprises. By now he was about seven years old and a habitual run away. Even stealing was not excluded from his bad behavior. He would be picked up by police in various cities and Mother would get notification to pick up her son at a police station and pay the train fare for his return. At one such incident she came armed with a wooden spoon in her purse to claim her unruly offspring, but the officers stopped her on the spot from doling out corporal punishment in their presence. The boy was no longer the cute little curly haired tot everyone adored at age three.

He was trouble on a daily basis. He took apart my only doll just to see what was inside, and also dismantled my harmonica, a present from my paternal grandparents. He could not be trusted to stay in school after being deposited there daily, so Mother had to put him into a home for boys, where he got excellent care, his meals and clean clothes to wear.

This new apartment came with strictly adhered to rules concerning the cleanliness of the building. Every 83-floor had two tenant families who were responsible to clean the two sets of granite stairs and a wooden landing. On our floor this chore was between the couple on the other end of the corridor and us, meaning me. The old ladies were exempt from this job for obvious reasons. Because of school and homework on Saturday's I had to clean the stairs and landing on Sundays. The granite stairs were easy to wash, but the wood floor on the landings had to be done on hands and knees with a scrub brush. The soapy water made the brush a bit slippery, and without a very tight grip my hand slid off the brush and I immediately received a splinter under my right middle finger. Ouch, that hurt like the devil, but I was able to remove that splinter fast enough and in one piece. The following Sunday I was not that lucky; a dark cloud must have hung over my head. Once again, as I was scrubbing the wooden landing with a brush and soapy water, my hand slid off the brush. As if it was meant to be, I got a very long splinter under the same finger nail. This time I was not able to just pull it out, instead only the protruding part broke off, while the rest remained imbedded under the nail and out of my reach. Mother send me straight off to the clinic with the reminder to meet her afterwards at her Aunt Ida and Uncle Franz's, the master tailor. It seems we had been invited to dinner on one of those rare occasions. After a short wait I was called into the doctor's treatment room. He had me sit opposite and facing him, took a look at my finger and called for two nurses. This got me just a little worried. As the doctor wedged my hand between his knees, the nurses, one on each side of me, held me down by my shoulders. With the pointiest pair of scissors, I ever saw, he cut a triangle up two thirds of that nail without the benefit of any numbing of that digit. At this point I would have welcomed an anesthesia. To say that I saw stars is putting it mildly. He removed that portion of the nail and the splinter, while I let out some ear shattering cries. There was no topical stuff to numb the finger, and in their mind not enough of a big deal to give me either to knock me out. To add insult to injury, I was asked to step behind a screen and drop my panties. Now what, I thought, as I received what they called a tetanus shot into my butt. Drawers up, skirt in place, I walked out of there silently congratulating myself for not having fainted while being tortured. I got to Aunt and Uncles apartment, rang the doorbell, Aunt Ida opened the door, and she just barely caught me as I fainted retroactively. So much for being proud. Dinner was great, because the availability of certain foods had become somewhat better. I always thought of Mothers Aunt Ida as a domestic wonder. After dinner she send me and Brother to their cubicle in the basement to select a jar of any preserved fruit for dessert. We could hardly believe our eyes, there were two shelves stocked with glasses of preserved pears and cherries and who knows what, we simply could not decide on what to take. Then we did something so unthinkable, the thought of which makes me feel guilty to this day. Karl-Heinz and I opened a jar of pear halves and ate them all on the spot. After replacing the rubber ring and metal top, we selected a jar of cherries to be our desert. The guilt I was feeling in the days and weeks to come did not leave me, yet I never mustered up the needed courage to face her. I never took the time in the years to come to apologize for our youthful transgression, but somehow, I feel she understood why we did it. Our mother just was not domestically inclined or willing to do anything that required work without instant gratification, or to just please others.

Mother was also not a fan of doing laundry to the point where I had to wear the same dress to school for more than a week. For that reason, no one would ever find a class picture with me in it. The same was true of my underwear. With hormones changing and not knowing what was going on with my body, I felt timid and ashamed when the crotch of my panties turned somewhat stiff due to discharge. I did not discuss this even with my best girlfriend in fear she would be disgusted by me. One day after school, about two weeks before my fifteenth birthday, I practically ran up the stairs to our landing and into the toilet, because nature called. I looked down and to my horror I saw a little bit of blood in my panty. I was at once certain I had a severe venereal disease and will bleed to death. Not wanting to tell Mother in fear of getting punished, I waited for the first opportunity to burn the panty when she was not home. The same fate awaited the second pair, but now I was afraid I would run out of undies. Just then came time for her to do laundry and she asked where the rest of my panties were. I burst into tears and confessed that I had burned them because I was going to die, in fact I was bleeding to death. At first, she looked a bit stunned, then realized what was happening and started to laugh until tears ran down her face. Not really understanding her reaction, I felt she did not have to be that happy about my impending demise. It was bad enough knowing she did not care enough to be at least a little bit sad that I had only a limited amount of time before dying. After she calmed down a bid, she told me this was a natural occurrence and would happen every month, and for that reason I needed to keep certain equipment on hand. Well, at least I was not going to die any time soon. At this time, I made a silent promise to myself: if I grow up, and if I should get married, if I had children and there were girls, I would make sure to educate them about some facts of growing up. There should be no reason to suffer such anxiety over nature's rules of growing up. Sure enough, the following month this happened again, so I ran into the nearest drug store and made the quickest U-turn ever, because there was a young man behind the counter. I would have been mortified to ask him for the female product, but Lothar was home for a week end visit, so I gave him a note and money and send him off to buy my so very personal items.

    Things were not exactly going smooth at school for me as far as our social studies class went. Communism was constantly hailed as the only form of government that would make life good for all. Our curriculum was completely about Russia and all other communist countries. This was not restricted just to the main cities, rivers and mountain ranges, but also about their products. We had to memorize in which region the wheat grew best and that the black sea area had sub-tropical climate that grew oranges. At this point I had never even seen an orange. We learned everything there was to know about most communist countries, to the point we even knew the middle names of Stalin and Lenin. I did not even know the middle name of either of my grandfathers. We had been told over and over again that the poor people of West Germany had no jobs, the stores were overfilled with American goods that no one could afford. My questions about us having ration cards and the goods that the ration cards named were mostly not available, fell on deaf ears during our social studies classes. Sometimes the lessons were so idiotic, I had every reason not to believe our teacher. Instead, the orders coming from Russia, oh pardon me, from the Soviet Union, were to Sovietize East Germany. By now we kids were already fluent in the Russian language, which Karl-Heinz and I used when Mother was not to hear our conversation. The year 1953 proved to be fraught with upheavals of the political kind.

One day in March, while at school, we received the news that Stalin had died. Of course, I knew he was a dictator with a nasty streak, therefore that was great news for me, but I did wonder what kind of new communist was going to take his place. The entire school was herded into the auditorium, where a huge picture of him hung on the wall with a black cloth draped around the frame. After a short speech about what a great man and communist leader he was, we had to stand for five minutes of silence to show our respect. They were the longest five minutes for a person I did not know personally, nor cared for any way. As I looked around and saw the teachers with their sad faces, as if a close relative had passed, I could not help thinking what hypocrites they must be. Surely, I was not the only person who questioned and despised the whole concept of that regime. For some reason I found the whole scene just a bit laughable and could not suppress a small giggle, that started deep in my belly region and worked its way up while getting louder and louder. I felt the elbows of my friends to my right and left in my ribs, accompanied by shushing sounds, which only made me laugh more, but now with both hands over my mouth in an attempt to muffle the sound. That was useless. We marched back to our classes in silence and waited for the teacher. There was the sound of a click in the schools intercom system, then the sound of a stern voice inviting me to report to the principal's office. Well, what can I say, I received a sermon on better behavior in public during important political functions. I tried to fake my way out of this one by explaining my behavior was due to nervousness and stress. After all, our idol had just died. Oh boy! I was good and surprised that I got away with that one.

On a day, when gym was our regularly scheduled activity, we were led into the school yard and met by a different teacher, who informed us we were going to learn how to shoot a rifle. The whole class was stunned at this news, and I could not believe they would actually teach young teens how to shoot a rifle. I was first in line, because everything was always done in alphabetical order. Usually I would have been second, but Altman was absent that day. The instructor told me to lie on my stomach on a wood chaise, without the cushions, and at the same time pressed a rifle into my hands. I was a bit stunned at this request and took a few moments to collect myself. Then I heard my voice say a loud "no" at which point he grabbed my arm and shoved me onto that lounge, with the rifle still in my hands. I heard the whole class gasp, and at that moment knew I was not going to shoot at the target he pointed out. I made the reason for not wanting to shoot a rifle very clear: girls are not drafted into the people's police (the East German excuse for having an army) plus there are no gun shops, so why do I need to learn how to shoot. While explaining this to him I had turned my body slightly to face him and inadvertently pointed the rifle at him. He yanked me off the chaise, most likely in fear that I might pull the trigger, then turned to call on the next student, also a girl, who stood there and was already dissolved in tears. The next class mate was a boy, who also refused to shoot with the explanation that he would be drafted as soon as we graduated, that would be the proper time to learn military activities. That teacher simply gave up, but without my knowledge I was somehow marked as a troublemaker, or worse. The word dissident came to mind.

In the meantime, we were informed about a class trip, or career day, to tour a factory in preparation to give some thought to the possibilities towards a future profession. I already knew my interests did not include becoming a hairdresser or typist. I had an aversion to touching other people's greasy hair, nor did I want to sit all day pounding a typewriter and learn the hieroglyphics that were called shorthand. My interests were leaning more towards teaching or being an opera singer, but those choices were not offered. Heck, in my younger years, while reading about Tom Mix, I even considered trying my hand at being an Indian fighter in America, or better yet a bull fighter in Spain. That colorful and tight fitting costume held a certain fascination and I did not think there existed a female bull fighter at that time. I could have had the distinction to be the first. My imagination had no boundaries but thought a more realistic choice might be in teaching, also not offered at that time. Instead, we got an introduction to several different machines and how they were operated, we even were allowed to try out some of them, naturally with some instructions from the workers who manned them. I was particularly impressed by a lathe I was able to try out. At the end of the tour and upon reaching the outskirts of our city, the teacher gave us free time to do as we pleased. A nearby soccer field had a game in full swing and a few of us decided to watch. As I got off the bike, which I borrowed from a friend of Mother's, my classmate behind me whispered to get back on my bike with great urgency in her voice. It appears I got my period during the ride back from the factory, so when I got off the bike at the stadium the whole seat of the bike was imprinted in blood on my dress. Needless to say, I raced home without stopping for anything, even a red traffic light. Darn, this was becoming more and more inconvenient and unannounced, no warning and no cramps. I guess I had to live with it from now on. Mother was at home when I arrived and I gushed about the factory visit and my decision to become a lathe operator. My enthusiasm was instantly squashed as she told me I was not going to work in a factory, but will be a pencil pusher, as she put it. This revelation stunned me for a moment, but then made complete sense: she actually wanted what was best for me. She did not want to see me work all my life at some dirty machine in a factory. She had informed herself of the fact that the company she worked for was going to have four places to fill for an apprenticeship program in technical/mechanical drafting and design. She actually got me an appointment for an interview in the engineering department, but from there on I was strictly on my own. With a hand written history of my just fifteen years on this planet and my mid-term grades from school, I seem to have impressed the head engineer and the teaching master sufficiently to secure the first of four spots of a three year program. With the signed papers in hand, I walked into class the next day and proudly showed my homeroom teacher, Mrs. Hansen, my contract. This was received with great enthusiasm, as I was the first student in my class to have secured such a prestigious position. This was obviously the first step in the right direction for a successful career for the rest of my life, providing I did well in all my studies. Yes, at this point I was rather proud of myself.

Suddenly, Mother received a telegram from my paternal grandfather stating that my paternal grandmother was in grave physical condition. Thinking the old dear was about to depart this planet, Mother secured a ten day leave to West Germany with me in tow. The telegram did the trick and off we went on an approximately six-hour train ride to "The West." I was so excited and could hardly wait to see my other grandmother as well as my grandpa. We found grandmamma, as I was instructed to call her, in the best of health, they just wanted to see their only grandchild. Oh yes, I remembered, Karl-Heinz had a different father, who was killed in World War II, as was mine. The welcome at grand mammas was warm with handshakes all around, a curtsy and a hug on my part. We had a lovely evening, a wonderful dinner and just before grandmamma retired to her room, she gave Mother and me a very small piece of chocolate. It took just enough time for the old lady to be out of earshot when Mother flew into a fierce, but hushed, tirade about my grandma's stinginess. "Can you believe this," she hissed in a low voice, "giving us this tiny piece of chocolate. Well, I'm going to have some more of that." She opened the cupboard where she saw that little green box had been placed, took it out and offered me some. I respectfully declined with the excuse that I was satisfied with what was offered to me, while Mother just about consumed most of the contents of the box. We said good night, I went to my small bedroom and fell into a deep sleep. Next morning, I heard voices that were not exactly sounding very friendly. My grandmother filled me in about what had transpired since she gave us the tiny piece of chocolate the night before, which was in actuality Ex-Lax, a medicinal way to regulate our bowels, since we were not used to the western culinary delights. But Mothers greediness once again took over, and grand mamma shouted, "and she suffered the consequences by sitting," she now raised her voice a bit, "with her behind over my kitchen sink, because she could not make it to the toilet." At this point Mother was scrubbing the sink for about the fourth time and it was clear to me that grandmamma knew my mother well. I smiled inwardly, because finally someone yelled at my mother and she did not talk back. It was a happy day for me, the ladies had made some peace with each other and were enjoying an afternoon coffee. I asked to be excused so I could take a walk to explore the area a little. It so happens I was about to pass a large department store but decided to enter and see what was available. I took up position close to a cash register for no other reason than to see what people were buying. My eyes were getting bigger by the minute as I watched the sales person ring up one item after the other. I heard the voice of our social studies teacher in my brain, insisting that the people in the west were mostly unemployed. A blatant lie, I thought, as a woman bought two pillows. I was reminded what women in the East had to go through for a pillow. First, they had to buy the ticking material and pay a seamstress to sew it in the precise dimensions of a pillow, the next purchase was the feathers. You could not get the cheapest grade, because the stems would often times poke through the fabric and pinch the head or face. Now I actually saw ready-made pillows, wow, and the clothes in a variety of colors and styles that looked festive, almost happy. Not like the mostly drab dresses in limited styles. It was not at all unusual to see more than one woman wearing the same type of dress and pass each other on the street. The only thought was about who looked better in that frock. I was overwhelmed and angry at the same time and actually looking forward to getting back to tell all my friends what I had witnessed while in the West. After only about four days with grandmamma we got ready to depart, because Mother wanted to get to Bavaria to have a visit with her sister Brigitta. She wanted to make the most of our ten day permit to stay in the West, so after Grandpa gave Mother a sufficient amount of money for the train tickets, we were off again. But to my surprise she informed me that our trek south would be by thumb, in other words we were going to hitchhike. If she did not have such a quick hand I would have refused to go along with her idea, and once again her love for money and her selfishness were demonstrated to the maximum. By train this trip would have taken most of the day, who knew how long it would take us to get from the Hamburg area in the north all the way to a small city right on the Austrian border. I was no longer looking forward to this adventure, as she called it.

 The first ride was in a truck and after a while I noticed the driver was putting his right hand on Mothers left thigh. A couple hundred kilometers later he pulled off the Autobahn on to a country road and made a stop to "stretch his legs." I got out as well to walk just about twenty feet away when I heard Mother protest loudly about something. I quickly ran back, got into the truck and noticed the driver now had a scowl on his face. Aha, I thought to myself, he got nowhere with her and was angry at this point. We continued in silence until we reached a small city, where he was to load some items into the truck. He said we should have some lunch and he would pick us up again to the next town, his last stop. We never saw him again. She was getting a bit weary and actually near tears, when a very well-dressed lady saw us standing there with our time worn suitcase. Mother informed her of our dilemma which got us an invite for lunch at her house nearby. She then commissioned her husband to drive us once again to the Autobahn, where it would be relatively easy to get another ride. Sure enough, this time a moving van stopped to pick us up. The driver was very nice and seemed to be glad to have company on this drive into the night. When he got near the exit where he had to leave the Autobahn he dropped us off at a rest stop, where the chances of getting another ride towards our destination was definitely better. By now it was almost one o'clock in the morning as Mother walked into the restaurant portion of the place. She instructed me to stay outside, this would be safer for me because of all the men inside. I really failed to see a safety factor in my remaining in darkness outside of a busy rest stop, but I figured she thought it might be easier to get the next ride without a teenager standing next to her. I had no time to think about what next, when a male voice asked what I was doing here. To my relief I saw he was a police officer who looked me up and down, most likely wondering what this young girl with no boobs, no hips and looking like a twelve or thirteen year old was doing here. With relief in my voice, I told him my mother is inside trying to get a ride. Wait here and I'll see what I can do he said and disappeared through the door. It was not long when he and Mother reappeared, followed by a somewhat older woman and her grown son. The officer had probably ordered them to give us a ride in their very nice BMW, they did not exactly look pleased. I was seated behind the driver and in no time at all I saw Mother had drifted off to sleep. I swear that woman could sleep on a picket fence. Not much later I heard the heavy breathing of the driver's mother and at the same time noticed his head getting a bit droopy. By now I was more than just a little concerned about his ability to drive and I was watching him closely. Sure enough, his head was tilted to the left and the car was following in the same direction. I raised myself off the seat to look over his shoulder, saw we were headed off the road, and without hesitation I shook his shoulders. His sudden correction awoke his mother, who insisted he should stop and walk around the car a few times. I felt at this point they should be very happy to have taken the hitchhikers along, otherwise they would have had a serious accident. Day was dawning, we had a few more uneventful rides, the last one being in a little Italian convertible that could barely make it up a hill. With four persons and luggage the car was over taxed and we got out to walk the rest of the way. We finally made it to Burghausen, a small city located on the border between Germany and Austria. The down town area had a charming medieval appearance and a most impressive looking fortress on top of a hill. The city just oozed charm and a beauty reminiscent of kings, lords and ladies of long ago, no wonder it was a desired tourist destination. "Tante" that is German for aunt, Brigitte was happy to greet us, plus there was another surprise, namely Tante Lotte was on a visit from America, where she lived with her husband, a former military man who was stationed in this area at wars end. They were married a number of years but did not have any children. In fact, my aunt was told by several doctors she would never have any, for that reason she wanted to bring someone from the family to the States. It appeared the choice might be me, if I ever finished school and had the chance to make it out of the East. That prospect might be something to strive for. The reunion of the three sisters held their attention that left time for me to explore this pretty town, walk up to the fortress and cross the drawbridge to the inner court yard. Wow, what a place, I just stood and stared at everything, and the view was breathtaking. The fact that everything looked friendly and inviting, in spite of the obvious age of these buildings, made me realize how drab and dreary our surroundings are in the East. Nothing had ever been cleaned or painted, all the buildings had the dirt and soot of the wartimes still on display, which had a direct and negative effect on the population. Even I was affected by the completely subdued behavior around me. One day I caught a reflection in a store window as I walked by and wondered who is that old lady beside me, she seemed obviously depressed. I stopped suddenly and realized there was no one else in sight that slightly bent forward person was me. No wonder Mother would ram her fist into my back with the command to walk straight. Oh! How I hated that. No wonder that I had thoughts of suicide not long ago. On my way home from school, and after walking up to the fifth floor, I grew weary at the thought of facing Mother, never quite knowing what mood she was in. While standing on the sill of the fifth-floor open window I had all intentions to jump. I looked down on the cobble stoned surface below, wondering if it would hurt much, or would I die of fright before hitting those stones. For just about a second I thought SHE would be sorry and sad, but some kind of reality smacked me on the brain and I knew she might just be happy to be rid of me. I was not going to do her that favor and got off the sill, just as Karl-Heinz came up the stairs and inquired what I was up to. Oh nothing, I replied, and we walked quietly towards the apartment to ascertain what mood she might be in.

While walking back from the fortress a young man greeted me and asked if he might walk a bit beside me. I thought it strange but figured in a small town where almost everyone knew each other the appearance of strangers was definitely something worth investigating, in a friendly way, of course. His first name was Ludwig, a rather old-fashioned name for these modern times, but his family name was of four syllables, a common thing in names of people in the south. The dialect was exactly what I thought was polish almost a decade ago, when we had evacuated to lower Bavaria. Yes indeed, I was once again in Bavaria and glad that my aunt had not yet let go of the High German language. Well, Ludwig and I chatted away with him asking where I was from, how long are we staying and may he invite me out to dinner. Well, that was a new one. Nobody had ever asked me out to eat. Did I suddenly blossom or appear pretty? I was aware of the absence of even a hint of breasts, so I did not think so, but the prospect of my first meal out was exciting. I told him he would have to ask Mother for permission to let me go out with him, he agreed. She was at first inclined to deny that request, but my two aunts urged her to let me go and enjoy an evening out. He took me to a very nice restaurant, where everyone knew him and did not hide the nosy stares in my direction as they greeted him. During our conversation I learned he had just finished his apprenticeship as a baker and pastry chef and was well on his way to earn a good living. Not bad, I thought, as I studied the menu and became aware that I had never had a whole piece of meat all to myself. There were so many things to choose from, but finally I decided on a pork chop and roasted potatoes. The meal was served on a lovely decorated plate, now armed with knife and fork I was ready to attack the meat. Inexperienced as I was, the knife slid off the meat and send half of a potato flying into my lap. Quick as lightning, I retrieved the wayward potato with my fingers and placed it back onto the plate, while Ludwig pretended not to have noticed any of this. It was obvious I had been sawing away at the bone instead of the meat, which was hidden by a coating of bread crumbs. At this point I was just mortified by my inexperience and clumsiness but elated that my date pretended not to notice anything out of order, he was a true gentleman. After leaving the restaurant we slowly strolled past a still open fruit stand, where Ludwig bought some grapes, cherries and pears for me. We said our good byes at the front door, he even kissed me twice briefly on the lips. I pulled away both times, because I really did not like the taste of him. I guess there was just no chemistry or my lack of inexperience. No, it was the taste. Too bad. The aunts thought it funny that I brought back all the fruits, Mother was pleased about getting something she did not pay for, of course. I wondered what became of the money grandmamma had given her for the train. I needed not wonder for long but found out very soon that she had bought herself some nice pieces of material that were to become two new dresses for her to wear at upcoming dances back home. Yes, our time was up, and we had to return home like Cinderella from the ball. The time to return to the East came much too soon, but this time we went by train, hitchhiking across the border was out of the question.

The first day back home was a school day, second period was social studies. I was not looking forward to this class and all the lies, which were by now confirmed as such by my short visit to the West. When that little gnome of a teacher, yes, he was no taller than maybe one inch compared to my height, started to lecture about the wonderful doctrine of Stalin, Lenin and how it provided us with our wonderful existence, I tried to be a model student, but just could not be silent any longer. His constant litany of lies was more than I could stand. I raised my hand to speak, rose from my seat as we always did out of respect to the teachers, and proceeded to tell every little detail of my experience in the West as the class sat silently listening. When I got to the point that all that was taught was nothing more than lies and propaganda, I suddenly noticed he was slowly approaching me. When his face was just about three inches from mine he hissed "you little Nazi", turned and left the class room in great haste, slamming the door behind him so hard that I feared the little window in the door would fall out. I wiped a tiny bid of spittle that landed on my cheek from my face with the back of my hand. For just about a moment, I was stunned by his outburst, not expecting such a strong reaction. I really wanted to say how dare you calling me a Nazi, I think you most likely were one, but he had retreated too quickly for that. Silence surrounded me while I was still standing, nobody said a word, and the shock of my little lecture was still on all my class mates faces. I was waiting for the aftershock I knew was coming. Sure, as the sun rises, after a few minutes the scratches, then click of the school intercom system directed me to appear at the principal's office. Different school, different principal, but the lecture was the same. However, that was not enough punishment for such a major attack of the system, nor the audacity to wrongly give such a report of our enemy to the whole class and the teacher. No, no, that would never do. Instead, they found the only way to get back at me was to take Mother's overtime away from her, with the explanation that she needs more time at home to raise her children better. You could not hurt her more than rob from her purse. Upon my return from school that day she was already primed and in such a rage, the blows were hitting me hard. I was not allowed to cry out, because the previous year our neighbor couple had reported her to the child welfare office about child abuse. I still remember the visit, one man and one woman, who told her we would be placed in foster care if the abuse were to continue. I also remembered Mother's order not to cry out or get several more severe blows. Sometimes I wished we had been placed with other people as our guardian, it could not have been worse.

    On the first work day I reported to the lobby of the factory, where I met the other three hopefuls. I was not the slightest bit surprised that we were all girls, most of the boys were drafted into the people's police, another word for army, which the East was not allowed to have. Unless they were physically unfit, and only then, the boys were allowed to occupy an office job. A bit shy at first as we introduced our selves to each other, I felt we should get along quite well, after all, we had to spend the next three years in each other's company, six days a week. There was Helga, who appeared a bit sophisticated and spoke well without any slang or local dialect, but her walk was something else. Either her hips were moving differently than ours, or it really was a bit of a waddle that earned her the nickname Wachtel, which is a female duck in the German language. Naturally we did not call her that to her face, it was merely a reference when talking about her. Next was Inge, the middle child of five girls, her father was obviously hoping for a boy. She was a bit shy and the tallest and skinniest girl I had ever met, and very uncomfortable about her height. I wished at once I had a few inches of her height. During all her school years she was therefore chosen each year to be send to some kind of health camp for two weeks during vacation time. Their attempt to fatten her up a little showed absolutely no results. Then there was Christa, my namesake. I disliked that name, because it was just too popular and I had every intention to change it once I was old enough. The "other" Christa was just a couple inches taller than me, which once again made me the shortest member of this newly formed quartet. Her friendly face and easy way led me to believe we could be very good friends, and I was not wrong in my assessment. Our curriculum for our first year was explained, and to our surprise we learned that we were not going to see any part of the drafting/engineering department for an entire year. No pencil pushing time in the office, wow. That time would be spent in the factory, one month in every department. We had to learn about what goes into the manufacture of any given article, in essence learning our craft from the ground up.

This could be interesting, I thought, wearing the grey smocks like all factory workers and getting just as dirty had a certain appeal, even though I hated wearing anything that was dirty. But this was different, a part of learning while earning a living. The fact that we were going to be paid during our apprenticeship made this look like a sweet deal. In our first year we would earn seventy-two east Marks per month, with slight raises during the second and third year. At this point I was sure the value of my existence on this planet went up by leaps and bounds. The week was again divided into three days of school and three days of work, on Saturdays until noon. On the first day of our class, I became aware that this opportunity was offered only to girls, simply because there was only one male student in our class. He appeared a bit soft and downright fluffy and was most likely rejected for military service. I noticed the same trend on the first day of work at the factory. Not that I did not see any male students, there were about twenty of them, but they were all learning skills as factory workers, such as sheet metal and on various machines, while those with lower test scores were sent to serve with the people's police.

Our first task was to secure a piece of steel in a vice and then file it down by about two millimeters and continuously measuring it with special calipers. The surface had to be completely level and filing it down took forever. The chore was boring as all get out, and so we would play little tricks on each other. Nothing severe, just enough to have a mild curse or a laugh. If one of us made a trip to the lavatory, one of the others would rub just a tiny bit of spit on the surface of the steel to be filed. This action would make the steel slippery and the file could easily slip off and land on the floor if you did not have a tight enough grip on it. Next, we learned how to make a chisel. I loved this part, for after filing the steel to the proper dimensions we got to place it in the fire, all the while having a tight grip on it with rather long tongs, until the piece was red hot. Then we hammered it on an anvil until we achieved a flat edge at one end, almost resembling a chisel, followed by dipping the still very hot piece into a bucket of water to harden the metal. This was great fun, until my smock caught fire as I held the tongue with the red hot metal too close to my side, while awaiting my turn at the water bucket. With the help and quick actions of the other Christa the damage to my smock was minimal and no damage to my body. Our master teacher most likely saw trouble ahead with four female students in his group, but he never lost his patience.

He also led a small band of harmonica players, which I joined, and I must confess we sounded pretty good. At the same time, I heard about a folk dancing group led by the third year students from the drafting department. This was great news for me and I could hardly wait to join the group. We had practice every Saturday evening and I made sure to learn every dance as fast as possible. After practice the whole group went to the nearby corner bar and cooled off with a beer, my choice being of the dark and slightly sweet variety. This well-ordered routine did not last long, because the older students were now ready to graduate, and some left the firm for jobs with other companies. To my sorrow this meant the old folk-dance group was now defunct. The dance group was sponsored by the communist party, they even supplied summer and winter costumes to be worn at performances for various communist functions, as well as at old age homes etc. We even had our own accordion player during our practice sessions, which proved to be so much easier than having to reset the old record player when we had to iron out mistakes. I always loved dancing as well as music and was thrilled to have been able to join all my favorite pastimes. At least this kept me away from the apartment at certain times when Mother was at home. All this activity did not remain unnoticed by certain zealous party members, who found out I was not yet a member, but taking advantage of all the perks that were offered by the communists. The third-year students were ready to graduate which left me as the only survivor of the dance group. I did not want to give this up and did my dandiest to try and recruit, as well as hold auditions for possibly talented dancers. What a mess, we needed at least four pairs for some of the dances, but finally got a complete troop. I had no problems getting girls to join, it proved much more difficult to convince an equal number of boys to give up some of their spare time. It appears once again I was watched or spied on and seriously pursued by the party to participate in their activities. I did the mandatory marching in some parades, but that was all I was willing to do at this time, claiming my studies were taking up a lot of my time. But with a big party event coming up shortly in Berlin, they most likely had their hands full with planning as to who should represent our city.

Bigger problems were looming on the horizon. A mandatory reduction in pay, yet higher level of productivity for all workers started a revolt by construction workers in Berlin and spread to the rest of East Germany. This happened to be a school day on which we were ordered to leave the building. The same occurred in the factory just next to the school. Not really knowing what was actually happening, we were soon swallowed up by the mass of people headed towards the center of the city. I noticed a teacher as well as our principal removing the communist pins from the lapel of their suits in fear of retaliation from the public. I was not able to break free from the mass of people and just let myself be swept away to who knows where. Of course, the Soviet Union found out about the uprising and orders came to immediately squelch this action by any means. By the time we reached a main plaza with an imposing brick building, that was actually the city jail, the doors had been forced open by the demonstrating mass, and many ragged looking men, half naked with just blankets draped around them, emerged. In all that haste I do not recall if any women prisoners left that building as well. At the same time a Russian tank came rolling down Main Street and proceeded to shoot one salvo over our heads and were not even trying to avoid squishing any one in their path. This attempt to rid ourselves of the soviet dominance was ended as fast as it had started and became known as the uprising of March 1953, then life continued as usual.

As luck would have it the harmonica club, as well as our folk dancing group, were selected to be a big part of the delegation to Berlin. This meant we had to perform at this big event and the excitement was enormous. Besides many practice sessions with both clubs, there were some briefings by party members on what not to do while in Berlin. We were told that during this very important international youth communist gathering the east-west border in Berlin would most likely be a bit relaxed. Under no circumstances were we to cross into the western section of Berlin. We were also warned that there were going to be men in trench coats stationed at the border crossings for the sole purpose of luring young people to the west. You would then be drugged and taken away, never to see your family members again. This tactic had the desired effect, namely, to scare all of us from even thinking about taking a little sidestep into the unknown, but deep down I did not believe any part of this story for a minute. I had already pondered why so many peoples deepest desire was to get to and live forever in the West, yet no one ever had the same urgent need to settle in the East. Anyway, the day of travel neared, I had packed my outfit for the performance with the harmonica club, which consisted of a black skirt and a white blouse that I had to borrow from a class mate. The dance costumes were colorful and very folksy and nice looking. Of course, the much lighter summer costume was to be worn. Our accommodations in Berlin were in the attics of row houses outfitted with mattresses and blankets and resembled a college dorm. The first day was filled with marching in a parade, then performances by the harmonicas, followed by folk dances and then some time off for us. The second day was almost like a repeat of the first and I grew more and more interested in finding out what the dreaded West was all about. I mentioned this to a close friend, who was appalled by the idea, but gave into her own curiosity, and promised to accompany me, if I was going to do this.

The next day, after a morning performance with the harmonica's, we had free time until late afternoon, so I decided it was time to have the adventure of a lifetime into the forbidden zone. The trains of the subway system in Berlin never completely stopped, instead they just slowed down enough for riders to gently hop off and on. What a neat idea, but I wondered how older people were dealing with that and not getting killed. This train was also not a subway in the truest sense, for it moved almost entirely at street level. We continued on the train until one stop past the border crossing, which was obvious by the wide corridor of what was called "no man's land", flanked by barbed wire on both sides and several high look-out towers in the middle. This bit of landscape looked about as menacing as it was meant to, leading to further thoughts of why you would want to cross that border anyway. We emerged from the train and walked up just a few steps to street level, when we were immediately greeted by two men wearing trench coats and hats, looking exactly the way we were told back home and how I imagined spies would look. For just a couple seconds I thought the commies were right, we are going to be abducted, as my friend took a couple hasty steps closer towards my side and making it look like we are attached at the hips. The men removed their hats and introduced themselves to us, assuring no harm was intended, indeed they were just extending friendly invitations for lunch. I was feeling a little hungry at that point and felt a little sandwich would be most welcomed. They told us we just missed the double decker bus that took other young people on a city tour. So, I thought, we are not the only escapees from the east, who gave in to find out what was on the other side, even if it was merely inspired by the growing sense of being nosey, and nothing more. How reassuring that I was not going to be the only one in trouble if we were found out, this time. The men led my friend and me to a villa only a few blocks from the station. We entered, and after a long corridor found ourselves in a huge room with an enormous table full of food, the likes I had never seen before. We were invited to take whatever we wanted. My eyes were just taking it all in before I could even think of what to taste first. There were luncheon meats of every kind, and some I had never seen before. There was so much fruit in abundance, but my eyes zeroed in on a pile of bananas I heard about but had never seen. So, I thought, is this how the poor west lives, or is this just another attempt to put us at ease before we were to be drugged and kidnapped? At this point I felt what the hell, if I'm to be abducted I will at least eat my fill and deal with the rest later. I suspected my friend must have had the same thought. We selected a wonderful plate full of goodies each, plus I chose a drink of juice that was of an orange color so bright, that I felt this could not be real. If this was poison, then I was going to die happy. Too soon we had to make our excuses to leave, I had a dance performance coming up and we could not wait for the bus that was to take us on a city tour. Before leaving we were urged to fill a plastic bag with whatever we decided to take with us, so we did, and I made sure I had selected at least one banana as well. As we sat in the train taking us back to the east zone, we realized the clear plastic bag was a dead giveaway about where we had been. We could not possibly take this back to our attic, and it would have been an enormous sin to just throw it away. So, we sat and ate everything from the bag before we reached our stop and felt unbelievably full while getting off the train. I did feel a bit off during the dancing performance, but I just scoffed it off to over eating. During the night I awoke in a sweat and enormous pain in my mid-section, my moaning also woke my friend and accomplice. She came to my bedside and asked what was wrong. The only thing I could think of was that the warning from the commies had come true. I have been poisoned and will die, that is the price I had to pay for my disobedience. I had to make peace with myself, good bye Mother (who will not be sorry, except there would be no more money for her), good bye Oma and Mommy Deen, I will miss them most of all. By one in the morning a doctor had to be summoned, who only agreed that I had a high fever but could not, or would not, tell what was wrong with me. After throwing up and passing out a few times, I did live through the night and participate, if not enjoy, the final activities of the day. Later on, we had to listen to the closing speeches by more communist big shots, who relentlessly reminded us about how lucky we were to live in the second best country in the world, the first, of course, being the Soviet Union. Then why, I kept thinking, is every ones dream to go and live in the West, but no one was anxious to come and live in the East. Of course, I knew the answer.

After returning to our city and the usual routine I found an envelope at my work station that contained an application to join the communist party. Aha, I have been found out taking advantage of all the nice things and activities that were offered and sponsored by the party without actually belonging. I dragged things out as much as possible, from not enough time to study and my little brother ripped the application, to I must have lost it. So, they went one little step further and invited me to a meeting at the party office, where I was told it would be to my benefit to join, for I displayed leadership qualities and could go far. I wondered if they were planning a political career for me, the thought was repulsive as I was only interested in a proper profession, the first step of which landed me in the factory. We went through several departments with good results and many compliments, the wood shop was great fun, so was working on a drill press and a lathe. At one particular machine, where a cutting tool would move vertically every second or two and remove a millimeter of metal at a time, Christa ll and I were assigned that particular post for the day. It was my job to constantly apply a lubricant that was a milky looking fluid. The whole setup was rather tall, and I was just guessing that my aim was sufficient. But Christa II was always helpful and found it necessary to perch on top of that apparatus. To make sure there was maximum lubrication where needed, she pushed the milky substance towards the edge to be cut. At one precise moment the cutting tool came down just as she pushed some escaped lubricant with her finger towards the cutting site, and it cut her right index finger from the first knuckle down her entire nail. As I saw her blood run down her hand and puddle on the machine, then on to the floor I immediately passed out. Some splatter of her blood was on my smock as well, therefore I was thought to be the injured person and was carried to the infirmary on a stretcher, while my buddy followed behind. I truly felt embarrassed about passing out so easily, but I never could stand the sight of blood, weather it was mine or other peoples. In between working in different departments, I finally joined the party and hoped they would now leave me be. The next part of the factory for us to work was the foundry, and I noticed our teaching master scratching his head and wearing a bit of a concerned expression on his face. I suppose he wondered what troubles lay ahead, not exactly unwarranted. We learned how to make forms with different types of sand, into which molten iron was poured on the days of scheduled smelting, usually on Saturdays, when we only worked half days. We got to watch as the liquid metal exited the huge oven via a long chute and into an enormous cauldron, all the while emitting white hot sparks that flew all around the area. I tried my hardest to avoid having any land on me, but the seasoned factory workers did not seem to be bothered at all. The air was very toxic on the days of smelting and usually made me nauseous. We could hardly wait to get out of that smelly environment and were usually in a great hurry. In my eagerness to be the first one out the door of the smelting department, I jumped over two rows of freshly poured forms, missing the last form by just a few inches. I just happened to look in the direction of our master teacher, who I knew was not in favor of taking short cuts and saw him turn white. When he saw me jump over the last form he must have feared that I touched the liquid metal, not yet solidified and cooled, with my foot and possibly burned it off. Luckily only part of the heel of my shoe burned off in an instant and I apologized to the master with all my heart. Several obvious dangers, plus the emitting toxic gasses made it possible to receive certain benefits. Therefore, all workers, who regularly worked in that department, received the highest ration cards in the system. They got whole milk, butter and more meat and other goods not available for other workers with less dangerous jobs. We four ladies felt very privileged to receive the same rations while working in the smelting department, except I felt a little cheated for not entirely getting to enjoy the benefits of my dangerous job. It was December, so Mother used most of the goodies to bake a cake and some cookies. I do not recall, but I hope I got to enjoy at least a little extra meat, maybe even some whole milk during that month, but I really doubt it.

One morning I decided to take a slightly different way to school, the reason for that was completely unclear to me. Instead of staying on the main street to the left, I took the ever so slight detour to the right, knowing the two streets would merge again just a couple blocks ahead. As I came to a building in the middle of the block a very strong smell of urine invaded my nostrils. I turned to see if some slob of a man, or a boy, was relieving himself, but there was no one in sight. I did not even detect a puddle on the side walk. This is very strange, I thought, but as I turned to continue on my way, I noticed a shiny brass plaque fastened on the stone front, next to the door of the building. It read "Orphanage of the city of Goerlitz". In an instant I saw the exact and complete layout of the interior in my mind. My goodness, I thought, now I'm obviously going crazy. Why would I even know what the interior of this building looked like, I certainly had never been inside. Just to ignore the image in my head did not work, I had to make sure I was not going crazy. I rang the doorbell and a white uniform wearing lady opened the door. She confirmed my knowledge of the various rooms, as I pointed with my index finger in the direction of their location. To her quizzical look I just said I must have been here at some point in my life and continued on my way. Yet the view of the dormitory style sleep room played like watching a movie in my head. There were two rows of approximately six cots on which we had to take a daily nap after the noon time meal. I recalled that I was never able to fall asleep, instead I just laid there looking around and hoping the time would pass faster. On the cot next to mine slept a little boy, who never failed to wet himself during his sleep. I remember hearing the sound of his pee trickling through the canvas of his cot and forming a puddle on the floor. So that was the unpleasant aroma wafting into my nose and invading my brain, but another surprise was the fact that I even remembered his name: Horst Klopstock. I was determined to make a quick visit to Oma after school, this was just too weird not to follow up on. I found it difficult to concentrate during classes and could hardly wait until the end of this school day. As per plan, I did go directly to Oma's apartment and told her about the most unusual happening while walking to school. I swear I felt her heart skipping a beat as she clutched one hand over her chest and placed the other on my shoulder.

"Oh my goodness, dear girl, I hoped you would never remember that time in your life," she said, "you were so little, after all, you were only three years old." I insisted she tell me the whole circumstances surrounding my being placed into an orphanage. Oma was not exactly eager to reveal all, but I pressed for the entire explanation, and she finally opened up on my urging for the truth. It appears Mother was always up for a good time, and I was obviously in her way and ruining her fun. The first time she abandoned me was in Hamburg, where she placed me with a couple who had no children. They may have had the intention of adopting me because I was already potty trained at age one. Mother returned to Goerlitz without me and avoided telling her father, my Opa Fritz, my whereabouts. Whenever he asked about me, she would have many excuses why he could not see me, until he forced the truth out of her. He actually went to Hamburg to collect me and found out the couple were relieved to get rid of me. It seems I missed my mommy and started wetting my panties, so they withheld all liquids and I was well on my way to dehydration. That was the first time Opa rescued me, the second was getting me out of the orphanage sometime after age three. Again, she had made many excuses about why she did not bring me to her parent's house for a visit. I was not surprised by any of these declarations of my past, because for the life of me I cannot remember ever having had a loving home life, nor did I ever receive a hug or a kiss from my mother.

Our "practical year" in the factory, as it was called, came to an end and the four of us girls were getting real anxious to begin the next phase of our training in the drafting/engineering department. After entering that huge room, with drawing boards lining three of the four walls, we met Mister S. who was to be our teacher for the next two years. He seemed like a nice man of a somewhat short stature, who could give a disapproving look that would command instant respect. The first thing I noticed was that everyone working here wore a white smock, like a lab coat. I got all giddy inside over the thought that we four would be wearing white lab coats as well, even though I thought they all looked like doctors. He then took us on a tour around the room, starting to the left of the entrance, to introduce us first to the senior engineer. We four were lined up like organ pipes with me, the shortest, at the front followed by Christa II, next was Helga, and Inge brought up the rear. This arrangement seemed quite natural, due to the fact that Inge was the shyer one in this group and would be followed in this order from now on. When shaking hands with strangers and older people I had been taught to also curtsy, which I did even at this point. I did so while greeting the other engineers, on to the designers and draftsmen, but did not curtsy when greeting the third-year students, after all, they were only three years older than I. After Mr. S's drawing board there were four desks placed flush against the wall and separated by four drawing boards, placed perpendicular to the wall. Mr. S. assigned us to the boards by what I thought was a random order. Not exactly, I discovered just a few short days later. It appeared to me that he liked females with boobs that is why Christa II got the board after his, because she had the biggest ones, next was Helga, whose charms were not far behind Christa's. Inge showed promise, where as I did not even have more than a slight hint of what might one day, in the distant future, appear. That is precisely why I ended up with the last board in the room, exactly opposite from the entrance to this enormous room. This suspicion of mine was confirmed solely by noticing his glances roaming occasionally from face to upper chest, particularly when he would be talking to Christa II. My habit to curtsy when meeting people did not go unnoticed by Mr. S. but was most irritating to Christa ll, who had decided to break me of that habit. After all, she did not want me to make the other three look bad, or maybe just her. After a couple weeks of my morning and evening curtsies she would follow very close behind me. Just as I was about to do this despicable thing with my legs she pushed her knee right into the back of my right knee, thus making me almost fall to the floor. Not wanting to appear to the rest of the office that I was about to cave in twice a day, I no longer curtsied. These little interactions did not escape the attention of our drafting master and must have given him the idea that the other Christa was a bad influence on me, big boobs or not. He therefore went directly down stairs into the factory where my mother worked. She, in turn, ordered me not to associate with that bad influence any more, but the two of them achieved just the opposite. We had become fast friends almost immediately and were going to stay that way forever. I found out much later that Christa ll's parents were not enthused about our friendship either, but for entirely different reasons. A single woman raising children was in their opinion not on the same socially accepted level. I believed that was their only reason for not wanting their daughter to associate with me. Our work day started at eight in the morning, with forty-five minutes for lunch and finished the day by five. Lunch time was always fun, we would go to the cafeteria and get a malt beer to complement our home-made lunches. The beer was of a deep brown color, with a slightly sweet taste and a little less alcohol content than the lighter colored beer. The factory workers would grin as we proudly walked back to our work stations, we knew they called our choice of drink mother's milk. Yes, in Germany workers were allowed to have beer from the cafeteria with their lunch and that custom, that was as old as the invention of beer itself, was never abused by the employees.

Along with the start of the second year of our apprenticeship came a most welcomed raise in salary. It jumped from 72 Marks per month to a whopping 85 Marks. In my enthusiasm I had expected to get a raise in my meager monthly allowance as well but was shot down as quickly as I voiced my request. When I pointed out the unfairness of just 5 Marks at this stage of my work, Mother told me I could keep all my money at the beginning of next month and would let me have my ration card as well. I could hardly believe my good fortune came to me without as much as an argument from her. Sure enough, on the first of the next month I got to keep my money, was handed my ration card, and for the first time I could shop for my food on my own. It became very obvious and embarrassing when I ran out of ration card after only two weeks into the month. For the duration of the remaining month, I lived on rye bread and marmalade, with not an inkling of help from Mother. After this fiasco, and a hard lesson in budgeting well learned, I gladly relinquished any former demands.

Upon entering the engineering department, I fully expected to jump right in and produce wonderfully accurate drawings, but to our big surprise we had to practice lettering for two solid months. At first, I felt slightly insulted at the thought that our master did not think we knew how to print, but then the complexity of this assignment sank in. The accurate norm set forth was that all lettering on drawings was to be at a seventy-two-degree slant. We had to print the entire alphabet at the prescribed slant, until it became second nature every time, we picked up a pencil. This seemed as tedious as the first month of filing on a piece of steel in the factory. After all that lettering was mastered, the drawing phase was sure to be fun, and the weekly routine of three times school and three times work continued. That routine was interrupted by a company dance party for all the workers on a Saturday night. Mother and I attended for some fun, and at one point a quiz show was announced. She urged me to participate because there would be a prize for the winner. I desperately hoped that I would not make a fool of myself, but found I was doing okay until the last question was asked. The moderator took just enough time for me to get real nervous, and then it came: what is the difference between a cutlet and a chop. My mind raced to the time I had dinner with Ludwig, when a half of a potato landed in my lap because I had no clue that a bone was hiding under all that breading. But now I knew, blurted it out and won a jar of frankfurters, much to the surprise of the audience. I was a star for fifteen seconds and Mother carried the precious winning as we left, in fear I might drop it. While dancing with one particular apprentice from the metal shop of the factory I noticed he had an eye on me. I liked him as well, and when he asked to walk me home I gladly said yes. Mother was still chatting with a couple coworkers, when Manfred and I started walking towards our apartment building. There was not much conversation going on, other than how pretty the moon looked and the mild temperature. As we neared the building, I was beginning to feel a little uneasy and downright queasy in my midsection. By the time we stood in front of the huge outside door I had full blown cramps. Walking up to the fifth floor to our apartment was out of the question, so a little more small talk was taking place at the door in front of the house. The cramps became worse to the point I was already stepping from one foot to the other. I even felt that something awful might happen at any moment but did not allow myself to think what that awful thing might be. Finally, we said good night and he leaned in to give me a kiss. He put his arms around me to prolong the kiss, which felt pleasantly warm and soft to the point where I almost forgot about the cramp in my insides. But as misfortune must have decided, that unpleasant feeling was not to be ignored, nature was now unmercifully in command. At this moment I felt like my interior was about to explode and I could not hold back the urge to ease the discomfort through flatulence, kiss or no kiss. All the tightening efforts of my stressed bottom region only made the situation worse, all control was lost and the inevitable happened. I cannot believe I actually blew a rather loud one at such an otherwise romantic moment, and in that most embarrassing of moments in my entire life I blurted out "I farted", to which he replied, "I heard". I saw my mother approaching, he departed and to my recollection I never had another date with him.

The first year in the engineering/drafting department, which was now the second year of my apprenticeship, went smooth as far as my future profession was concerned. However, on the political front things were beginning to heat up steadily and got to be shakier than ever. I had joined the communists a while back, but just being a card carrying and dues paying member was not enough for them. Now they wanted to get their hooks into and mold me to their liking. They had already taken Mothers overtime away and made her join the women's division of the party, alas not entirely with their anticipated results. A new and more drastic strategy was put into place that was sure to make me to see the errors of my ways. At this point I had finished 2 ½ years of my 3-year apprenticeship program and I was suddenly getting an unusually low grade on a paper I handed in at school, even though I knew it was a good one. Just days later the same experience happened at work. My drafting master, Mr. S, told me the drawing I handed in on that day was unacceptable and demanded I do it over again. To say I was surprised would have been a big understatement at this moment. I was completely perplex and my face, of this I am sure, must have shown it. I was sure my work was at the very least good and could not find anything wrong with it. Either he took pity on me, or his sense of fairness kicked in, but he took me aside and out of the possibility for others to hear any part of the following conversation. He informed me that a high-ranking party member gave him the order not to give me any passing grades on any of my work handed in from now on. I was so shocked at this news; my mouth must have dropped or my usually rosy color went a few shades toward grey. He gave me the good advice to at least fake some eagerness towards the party. That way I would be sure to graduate with good grades, otherwise fail at work as well as in school and wind up without a profession and three years of my life completely wasted. That was good advice, but most of all I appreciated his taking the time as well as the risk to inform me of my options. He could have easily lost his job by telling me this and making a somewhat underhanded suggestion. Easier said than done, but I had to mull it over carefully and then take the appropriate steps, after all... This was about my future and my entire life. After work I ran home, much to the surprise of my three friends who were eager to ask what the conversation with our boss was about. All the way home I was thinking about the awful possibility of not graduating, what would my life look like from then on, without a profession and zero chance to earn a proper amount of money to pay for just the most meager necessities of a guaranteed miserable existence. By now I was really feeling sick about this predicament. It did not take very long to decide on the only option, in fact it seemed like the only choice open to me. It almost made me sick to my stomach, but it took exactly forty-eight hours of brain wracking thoughts about any and all of my possible options. As scary as my possible decision seemed, I came to the conclusion that I had to leave this oppressive environment. My brain screamed leave, not just the city, that would fix nothing, but the country. That thought momentarily scared me almost out of my mind, as I realized my leaving actually did involve making my way to another country. Ever since the end of the war Germany was split in two and thought of as two different countries, with the East ruled by Russia and the West by America in the south, and Britain in the north. Further thoughts about this decision made me realize it WAS the only option open for me. How am I going about this, and where do I start? My mind was in such turmoil, my stomach constricted at once into what felt like a huge knot. At this point I felt a bit lightheaded, accompanied by the need to vomit, which I knew was induced by my own feeling of fear. The realization that I was not quite as tough as I thought I had grown to be, stared me in the face. A few sips of cold water pushed the sense of fear out of my mind, and I actually started to embrace the positive thoughts of what needed to be done next. All at once I knew that I needed some help from my three dear friends. Could I trust them with the knowledge of my planned actions and not betray me? We four had been thick as thieves for two and a half years and everyone knew if they saw one of us the other three were not far behind. At this point I just had to trust them, come what may.

The decision was clear, my friends had to help in various ways, because I was aware I could never do all the necessary preparations by myself without attracting some attention. Mother was working the late shift this week that meant she would leave the house by three fifteen in the afternoon and return home about one in the morning. Timewise conditions were perfect, I just wished this did not have to be done during the month of February, in the midst of winter, but circumstances demanded action now, not months from now. The next day, a school day, I called for a meeting at my apartment right after the last class. The girls did not know what to make of that request, we never ever got together at my place, but realized this must be something big. Well, I informed them of my plans and the reaction was exactly what I had imagined or expected. First was a round of disbelief, followed by no way, you are not going to do that. What if you get caught, the punishment would be great, and your life would be down the tubes. The consensus was not to even attempt this, but I stood firm on my decision. After their assurance and oath under penalty of death not to utter a word of the plan to anyone, I assigned the three most necessary tasks to be performed. I suppose by now a touch of paranoia may have set in, but I was not willing to do any of these three jobs in fear I might be found out. Helga was the most business-like person to go to the bank where I had a savings account. During the two and a half years of my apprenticeship with yearly increases in salary and concentrating on learning what was to be my profession, Mother never gave me more than the usual five marks of my monthly salary. There was nothing to buy for that amount, therefore I had decided to save for an eventual big-ticket item. Armed with a hand written note to the teller, explaining that I was too ill to be there in person, Helga was my best and trusted friend to close out my account. So done, she was then to give Inge enough money to get a train ticket to Berlin, one way of course. I really had no clue where else to attempt to cross the border except in Berlin, never knowing how many people had been shot or caught trying to do exactly what I had in mind. The third task fell on Christa ll, who had to buy a suitcase for my journey without any input of proper dimensions. I checked the ticket and found out the train left at three sixteen the following morning. I had never been up at that ungodly hour in the middle of the night, except for the nightly air raids at age five and six, but this was urgent, and I was to arrive in Berlin at eight in the morning. The suitcase was kind of cute, but I would have preferred another color. It was made of green and white speckled papier mâché, plus I was not sure if the items I wanted to pack would fit. After all the purchases I still had eleven marks left, but my friends were still not convinced I was really leaving. We'll see you in school tomorrow, they said amidst hugs and good night wishes as they left the apartment still in disbelief. My thoughts turned to getting started and deciding what to pack. First and foremost of importance were all of my school and work related documents, my apprenticeship contract, and last just a few items of clothes, if anything was actually clean. I did rustle up a skirt and one sweater, a blouse, two undershirts and a couple panties, nothing more was going to fit anyway. Some more papers and my drafting tools filled up my brief case, and my purse contained my wallet with the remaining eleven marks, as well as my only form of personal identification, that looked like a little passport which everyone got as of the sixteenth birthday. Now I had to figure out where to hide the suitcase, because it did not fit under the too low bed and the wardrobe did not have enough space. The only solution was to place it in bed with me, at the foot end, and smoothed the covers to hide the telltale bump. This worked actually very well, now the only thing left to do was to set the alarm for two o'clock and lay my clothes in a way, so I could dress easily and quietly in the dark without waking my brother. Of course neither he, nor any other family member knew of my plans, and I was absolutely certain that my mother would have never allowed me to leave, because it meant a loss of income to her. To my surprise I had no trouble falling asleep, the bigger surprise was being shaken awake by Mother, who heard the alarm go off from across the hallway and past the kitchen as she was about to turn in for the night. She wanted to know why the alarm went off in the middle of the night and accepted my excuse of having made a mistake. Wow, that was a close one I thought to myself, I would most likely have slept right through and missed the train to Berlin, but one moment later my heart jumped out of its usual place in my chest and into my throat, and I thought I would pass out. While resetting my alarm to the proper time for school Mother sat on the side of my bed barely missing the corner of the suitcase. All I could do was hold my breath until she was done and rose to leave the room. Now I was wide awake and anxious to make my getaway. Slowly I slipped out of bed, across the hall and into the dark kitchen in order to listen if she was in bed in the living room. Then her voice demanded what I was doing up at this hour, to which I just replied that I needed a drink of water. By now I hoped she would drift off to sleep fast since time was getting to concern me. I dressed, removed the suitcase from the bed and waited minute after precious minute. Finally I decided it is now or never, left the bedroom on tip toes, closing the door ever so carefully behind me, and as I tip toed ever so carefully towards the apartment door, I heard every miserable floor board creak its own muffled tune. I was sure Mother heard this noise, but I was going to bolt if I heard her voice once more. I maneuvered the first flight of steps down cautiously, after that my tempo picked up steadily. Once outside in the cold February night air I had to move quickly if I was going to catch that train. Finally I reached Main Street that led straight to the train station, my suitcase felt heavier and heavier by now, plus the handle had begun to squeak with every step. Way too many books I thought, but must push on. Then I heard it. A most uneven gait seemed to follow me on the opposite side of the street. It sounded like step plop, step plop, that came closer and closer. Now I knew I was found out, a sharp voice commanding me to stop was going to sound any second now. The step plop was now crossing the street towards my side and a rather friendly man's voice said matter of fact like, if I wanted to make the three sixteen train I better pick up some speed. He noticed I was struggling a bit with my suitcase and took it from me, at the same time handed me his briefcase, now we were really moving. In the meantime I noticed his strange walk was due to the fact he had a club foot. As a handicapped person he had the privilege to ride the train in second class, where the seats were upholstered and finished in plush velour fabric. He invited me as his guest to take a seat next to him, but reminded me after he got off the train a few stops before Berlin I would have to return to the class per my ticket. No problem, I thought, I'll be happy to comply. The day was dawning, it got lighter and lighter outside the train window. The nice gentleman reached his destination and left the train, and I made my way to third class and hard wooden bench seats. It took a while before I found an empty seat, it seemed like half the country was on the move. Finally, the loudspeaker announced the arrival at the main station in Berlin. Well, so far so good, but what next? My last visit to Berlin was two years ago for the communist extravaganza and that unorthodox visit per subway to the western sector. My plan was to replicate that former adventure, only this time there would not be any men in trench coats and hats to welcome me. With a certain amount of determination and an equal amount of very mixed feelings I got a ticket for the most important subway ride of my life, even though the train never went underground. I chose a seat in the middle of the car but pushed my suitcase under the seat opposite mine. For some reason that made sense to me at that time and was meant to not advertise my intent to commit an unlawful, even treasonable act. The train stopped briefly at the next few stations and each time several passengers would get off to go about their business. Then a loudspeaker would announce the name of the next stop and the fact that it was only three stops from the border. Within just a few minutes the most unpleasant voice over the loudspeaker informed all riders that this would be the next to last stop in the East and urged the riders to prepare to exit the train promptly. By now my heart was beating double time, the next stop was the anticipated last one before the border. The uncertainty of what would happen next gave me an unwanted dose of fear that spread from my brain along the main arteries and into the extremities. I suppose I could have exited the train at the next and last stop, hop on one going in the opposite direction and back to an uncertain future. No, no, no, that was not what this undertaking was all about. Instead, I summoned my last bit of optimism and the will to change what had to be changed, as well as a good portion of stubborn pride in myself. My wandering thoughts were interrupted by that unpleasant voice over the loudspeaker again, and this time it was urging Eastern residents to exit the train, after it had come to a complete halt. I noticed only one person, a man, sitting a few rows forward of my seat, but never dared to look behind me to check if anyone else was still in this car. Then two uniformed men, looking very much like soldiers, entered through the forward door, and judging by the sound, two others were also entering through a door behind me. I really wanted to check which team was going to reach me first, but instead I sat rigidly upright and tried hard to remain calm while observing the two in front of me.

In an instant I knew they were the border patrol with a known nasty disposition. One was holding a clip board and demanding specific papers from the man in front of me in a very clipped voice, while the other stood with an automatic rifle poised and at the ready, in case a situation arose. It was definitely a cold February day, but I detected with certainty that my armpits were getting moist. Mr. Clipboard stamped some documents and abruptly returned them to the man, then turned and approached me. My brain was racing as he demanded passport, an ID and travel permit in a no nonsense and harsh way. I had NONE of the documents he wanted to see, and I tried hard not to make eye contact with him. Instead, I observed the ever so slow motion of the machine gun being raised and pointed at my face, while Mr. Clipboard repeated his demands in measurably louder decibels. I guess he must have thought I was hard of hearing, but I just kept sitting still as I felt a river of perspiration flow down the back of my spine to the waist top of my panties. Some of it spread along the waist to the left and right, while some kept running down into my butt crack. I was pretty sure there was no evidence of fear or sweat on my face, as Mr. Clipboard made another attempt to get some reaction out of me by shouting his demands this time. I just kept a sharp eye on the gun, hoping that guy was not getting all worked up and shoot me, while I was so close to freedom. I also wondered at this time if it was possible for a person to die from fright. I certainly was scared enough for three people and tried hard not to show it. Suddenly the train jerked forward and was actually picking up speed rather fast. The two border guards regained their footing, looked at each other and raced towards the door behind me, then jumped onto the platform. They were also not allowed to cross to the other side or be charged with attempted desertion. To my surprise the guard with the gun was still pointing it at me from the platform through the closed window until we were out of sight. I felt he knew what was happening and might have wanted to end my journey right then and there, possibly out of jealousy. In another moment my thoughts were turned to the changing landscape that opened before me. We were actually riding through no man's land, a wide border section with a high wall of rolled up barbed wire and high lookout towers, that were outfitted with machine guns and soldiers who, I guessed, knew how to use them. It looked like a potential war zone, and we had heard that several people had died in these areas while trying to escape into the West. I also noticed at least one German shepherd dog patrolling the area. Next came another wall of barbed wire, and finally West Berlin, my freedom, and the hope for a good future. All of a sudden, I felt a hand on my left shoulder from behind me and a ladies voice said "congratulations on your successful escape from the East." I turned to see who was making this assumption, after all I did look inconspicuous, or did I? My attire was a rather drab affair. The tailored coat with its stand up collar in forest green had a rather military look to it. The fake leather ankle boots and shoulder bag in the same dark green hue I imagined made me look like a Russian commissar's daughter. It's a wonder I did not get shot by Mr. Clipboard's accomplice. The lady looked like a dowager queen, elegantly dressed, wearing a hat and a mink stole with the snout of the mink holding its tail for a closure, so it would not slip off her shoulders. That, I thought to myself, was classy and would never be seen in the East. But I said to her "whatever do you mean," to which she replied, it was very obvious I had just crossed the border. She also mentioned that in all the years of her travels back and forth she had never been witness to a successful escape. She wished me good luck in all my endeavors and I started wondering as to how long I should ride on this train before getting off. I had no clue where I was and decided on two more stops, then get off and on to the next step of my travels. Wow, I grinned to myself with great satisfaction, I did it.

    I stood on the side walk and tried to decide about going to the right or to the left, when I spotted a police officer in the most handsome uniform I had ever seen. I approached him and noticed he was very tall and had a friendly face. I greeted him with my most sincere "good morning" and asked what my next step should be since I had just crossed the border and needed some......Before I got to finish my sentence he threw his arms around my middle and gave me the biggest bear hug of my life, as I felt my feet dangle in midair. It was a wonderful feeling and a great way to be greeted, and I at once felt warm and welcomed by a stranger in a strange city. He dug into his pockets and gave me all of his change, along with a slip of paper on which he scribbled instructions on what bus to take and when to change busses. He wanted to make sure I asked for a transfer from one bus to the next, or I would have to pay again. I thanked him and followed his instructions until I reached the place where I was going to be processed. I looked at an inconspicuous office building and then at my wrist watch to see what time it was. It was around eight thirty in the morning and normally my stomach would have told me that I was missing a meal around this time. But I was too excited to even think of eating, so I entered the building and found myself in a long corridor with several doors leading into what you might call interrogation rooms. In the first room I was asked all about personal data, what made me take the risk to cross the border etc. It was made very clear that if my actions were simply because I had an argument with my mother, or any other trivial reasons, I stood a strong chance to be send back to my home city. After establishing much stronger than just personal reasons for leaving the East, I was able to assure the person asking the multitude of questions that my reasons were not entirely of a personal, but more importantly of a political nature. It appeared to me that these people might not have a clue as to the importance that politics played, which had a monumental effect on one's personal success in life. I was led to another room with another person who asked more questions. This time I was asked about any knowledge of Russian troop presence, were there any barracks and their location, about how many troops are in the area. Since I had absolutely no idea as to how many people make up a troop, I'm afraid I was not all that helpful in this area of questioning. They were, however, interested to learn about the many tactics used leading up to my not so difficult decision to exit the DDR, the Deutsche Democratic Republic, as it was called. This whole procedure took until about four o'clock in the afternoon, at which time I was instructed to report to an address in a suburban part of West Berlin called Frohnau. They even gave me proper bus fare.

The building was a large villa that had been turned into a girl's home for minors only. Yup, I was still a minor at seventeen, and received by the head lady of the facility, whom I almost immediately nicknamed Holy Marie. She looked strict and unyielding, yet she wore a smile most of the time. There were approximately eight other girls, mostly run away or troubled local girls, but four of us were actually from the East. One was sure to be send back because she was a thief, who had stolen money and her mother's wedding ring, then pretended to be engaged. I suspect that she was the one who stole my watch, though I could not prove it and the two policemen were unable to find it when I summoned them, much to the dismay of Holy Mary. After all she had to protect the reputation of the home, and the arrival of a lit-up police car was not welcomed. I probably should have let her handle the situation and possibly gotten my watch back, my first and very treasured item from my paternal grandparents. How am I going to explain that loss to them without appearing unreliable? Oh yeah, that girl was going back to face the music. All of us had chores assigned, they included peeling potatoes and preparing vegetables for the main meal, as well as shoveling snow and keeping our dorm room clean. Since I had my paternal grandparent's assurance from two years ago to take me in, I expected to leave Berlin soon. First of all, I had to let my mother know where I was, surely, she must be wondering by now what happened to me. I composed a very nice letter informing her about what I had accomplished thus far, but most of all I wanted her written permission to stay in the West since I was still a minor. After all I had done so far, I did not relish the thought of her demanding my return, and worse of all the sermons and admonishment from teachers and the party leaders. Well, it appears that "Holy Mary" also mailed a letter to mother asking what was to be done with me next. She must have figured out how many days the mail took to reach my mother and how many more days before she could expect an answer from her. The answer came much too soon in her estimation, which made Holy Mary suspect that I wrote a letter before she did, and immediately accused me of coercing Mother into granting permission for me to stay. It took me some time to convince H.M. that my mother would not be coerced by any one person, and that included the Pope. Besides, I was not informed that writing a simple letter to make the family aware of my current whereabouts, was taboo. Okay, for now I was once more in the clear. Two other girls and I were now called walkers, because we had to walk to several government offices over the next few weeks to get processed through a maze of paperwork. Many of the questions had been answered at previous times, but I guessed it was a method to check the validity of previous answers.

Next followed a trip to a doctor for a chest ex-ray as well as an exam from head to toes. I had never been looked at from so many angles and at so many places. The most embarrassing thing was a message from the doctor to H.M., who in turn was to inform us three that we needed to practice better bottom hygiene. I felt so embarrassed at the thought the doc could possibly have meant me instead of one of the others, or all three of us. The toilet paper in the East was of a crepe paper quality and therefore most uncomfortable, if not outright painful at times. Anyway, from that day on I made sure I did pay extra attention to my butt. After residing five full weeks in West Berlin, I got the news that I was finally being transported to West Germany. My excitement was enormous, especially after learning about the mode of transportation. I was actually being flown from Berlin to Hannover, wow. Of course, at that time there was no other way to get from West Berlin to West Germany, because the city was located in the middle of East Germany, with no permission or chance for ground transportation. Therefore, flying out of the city was the only solution, due to an internationally mandated air corridor. I hope I got that right. Anyway, my excitement was greater than I could put into words.

On the scheduled day of my flight, I was brought to Tempelhof airport. After all legalities were successfully performed, I walked out onto the tarmac feeling like a movie star. On that short walk toward the plane, I looked all around me, hoping the whole world was watching as I silently bid farewell to a sun drenched Berlin, in anticipation of another taste of freedom. My little papier mâché suitcase did not feel nearly as heavy at this time, although it contained the same amount and then some. I certainly did not need any help to carry it to the plane at this time. The flight was absolutely exhilarating and felt like everything I imagined it to be. But who knew those fluffy white clouds were full of dangerous turbulence, and who knew that there was always bright sunshine above even the greyest clouds. Not demure little me, nor at this point little traveled me, that's for sure. I could not keep from looking out of the window and admiring the landscape below.

But suddenly there was the voice of a flight attendant again, bringing me to the present and my dinner. By this time I was a bit hungry and ate with gusto every bit of what was offered, before going back in time and continuing the almost saga like story of my past so far. I picked up where I had left off, namely my first flight ever from Berlin to Hannover, and thinking it was way too short.

We landed in Hannover, where a bus took me on a rather lengthy drive to a most sinister looking encampment that was surrounded by lots of barbed wire. It had the appearance of a prisoner of war facility I imagined was most likely crowded with escapees from the East when "getting out" may have been a little easier. At the time of my arrival, it did not seem all that crowded, yet there was a busy schedule ahead. It started again with questions of why and how I left the East, followed by more physical exams. At this point I was most ill at ease at the thought of having an exam of the most private region of my body. To lay on the examining table without my panties on AND opening my legs was not going to happen. When the doctor approached with some kind of thin, long metal item in his hand I jumped off the table and a short chase ensued. I was subdued and then held down by two nurses and the doctor, who assured no harm was intended. I did feel a slight ticklish sensation in the lower abdominal region, while the doc did whatever he had to do. My panic subsided and the whole drama was over in relatively short time, but the trauma of that experience lingered on for a number of years. Let's face it, a female exam is not something a seventeen-year-old of my, or any generation, is looking forward to, nor was it by any stretch of the imagination anything other than demeaning. My stay at this refugee camp was a mere three weeks, during which time I became a citizen of West Germany without any pomp or celebration. But a new feeling of a certain amount, and much stronger safety was surrounding me at this point. Now I was getting very excited to finally be welcomed by my paternal grandparents.

The train ride to Lüneburg was rather uneventful, but the city itself is very beautiful, with a long history and a preferred destination for its health spas and mud baths. It turns out the city sits on one of the largest salt deposits, therefore its main industry is the very active Saline facility. The country side surrounding Lüneburg is known for the large meadows of beautiful heather, transforming the area into a carpet of purple when in bloom. All this was to be explored much later, but first I could hardly wait to once again get reacquainted with my grandparents, the parents of my father, who died during WWll on the Russian front. The way from the train station to their apartment building was still known to me from the short visit two years prior. Our greeting was heartfelt, though a little stifled. A visit is of short duration but moving in could have a forced permanence. To my inner self I promised to be as little bother as possible and help out as much as I could. Opa, as I was allowed to call grandfather, was a not very tall but rotund presence, with a booming voice, not unlike Winston Churchill. When he spoke, people listened. I was completely infatuated with his worldliness, his two trips around the world in a sail boat and fluency in five languages. Before the war he owned a large hotel and restaurant in Hamburg that was bombed and reduced to rubble, which was the reason they wound up in the smaller city and current residence. Grandmama, as I had been instructed to call her, had the appearance of a grand dame and dressed accordingly. It was immediately clear she was used to bigger and more befitting surroundings.

When they first arrived in Lüneburg, after being bombed out in Hamburg, Opa had purchased a more modest hotel and restaurant named "Heidkrug" am Sande. I actually remember having visited there for a short time, during summer vacation, when I was approximately ten years of age, and was completely impressed with their luxurious lifestyle. Opa had a complete staff of people for the hotel and restaurant, but Grandmama did some of the cooking just for the two of them. The moment I joined them I had a maid all to myself, a young lady from Poland named Meta. She had to ready my bath and lay out the clothes for the day, even do my hair so I looked proper when appearing at the breakfast table. I felt like a princess and hoped with all my heart this time would never end.

Well it did, and getting back to Mother was a harsher look at reality than before.

Getting back to the present, this small yet elegantly furnish with some antiques apartment, in this approximately five-hundred-year-old house, surely was not her first choice. It had me wonder how she maneuvered going up and down the wooden stairs that were so narrow you had to place your feet sideways. Even I had to be very careful not to tumble down head over heels whenever I left and returned, but she never complained and always remained the lady. On occasional days she asked me to accompany her on her walk, but the slow pace at which she moved proved to be a test to my patience.

It became obvious that it would take a while to locate a manufacturing facility that was willing to pick up where I put a sudden halt on my apprenticeship contract. I knew I had to be a little patient in my search, but knew it would be worth the outcome, namely finishing the studies for my future profession. In the meantime, I was willing to take on any kind of a job where I could earn a decent living wage and not depend on the kindness of my grandparents. This brought me to the household of a doctor's family, where I was to perform light chores such as dusting, vacuuming, making beds and doing the dishes. That was easy enough, since I did most of this back home since age ten, plus the doctors' residence was within walking distance. That was another point to think about and solve, in the event there would be a greater distance to tackle when I got back into a "real job", as I called it. My patience paid off after just about four or five months working at the doctor's household, when I was able to find, apply and get hired as an apprentice to finish my original studies. But instead of just finishing the last six months I had to sign the contract for nine months. This made total sense once I thought about the time line, which had to coincide with the school and graduating classes before summer vacations started. The firm was named Loewe Pump Manufacturing Co. that made any type of pumps for any kind of liquid and was located on the outskirts of the city. My getting hired made me the very first female ever to be employed in the drafting and design department by this company. This made me very proud, and I knew I had to do my best to prove I was worthy of this position.

The only mode of transportation to consider at my age and limited finances would have to be a bicycle. With my Grandfather as an advisor on such an important purchase, we headed to the most reputable bike shop in the city. I picked a pretty blue one, as that was my favorite color at the time. The price was a nifty 198.00 Marks, but all I had to my name was 49.00 Marks. My 48. Marks down payment left me with just one Mark for the rest of the month, Grandfather co-signed for my purchase, but his signature came with a lengthy sermon in the best Churchill-like voice. It was all about me better not thinking he would pay if I defaulted. If I was not making 50.00 Mark payments for the next three months, the bike was going to be repossessed. True to my promise, I was the proud owner of the bike after three months of diligent payments. This was possible only due to the fact that I was still living with my Grandparents during this time, or I would not have been able to afford rent, food and those payments, since I was only earning 99.00 Marks per month. With my transportation requirements solved I needed to look for a better housing solution, since Grandmama kept complaining about having her much needed rest disturbed in the morning hours. It appears that my moving the bike from the hallway to the great outdoors was not entirely without some little bangs or dings, which disturbed her rest way too early. I suppose having a teen living in the same space after decades of silent bliss was just a bit too much to deal with. Naturally, I understood their dilemma and found the perfect solution, namely a home for girls in the center of the city. This place was only available for as long as the girls residing there were full time students or in an apprenticeship program. Once again, the woman in charge was very strict and made all of us adhere to the ten p.m. curfew. She immediately reminded me of "Holy Mary" in Berlin, so I secretly named her Mother Superior, or M.S. for short. At first, I shared a room with another girl, but she was homesick and left the facility soon after I moved in. M.S. conducted nightly bed checks and discovered I was sleeping in my underwear. Well, she was not in favor of that and demanded that I should sew a night gown or pajamas. I was no shining star in our home economics class years prior, therefore the thought of sewing was not embraced with enthusiasm on my part. The thought of buying some night wear was perceived as an affront to her sensitivity, so off I went to buy material for my pj's to be. As a last show of resistance for this forced labor I chose stripes to insinuate prison garb. The bottoms turned out okay if you were able to overlook that one pant leg was just a tad longer than the other. The top was a different challenge. To simplify the task, I just cut a V-neck for ease of entry and dismissed the sleeves all together. That worked for me, and M.S. was not exactly pleased, but for now accepting.

Suddenly I became the most popular person at the home. It seems that dear Grandmama was not feeling her best, so my presence, much to my dismay, was desperately needed at Opa's establishment. This did not fit into my schedule at all. Cramming for final exams at school and work already put a dent into my social life but working for Opa after work with just a little time for a bite to eat, really was not in my plan. But being the ever-respectful person towards my Elders I accepted the task. He informed M.S. of my new duties until one a.m. each day, adding that I would have a body guard walking me home at that hour of the night. She was pleased with his concern for my safety and gladly accepted the bribe in form of a very nice bottle of liquor. This entitled me to the most sought after and rare opportunity of possessing a key to the girls home, hence the popularity. They all thought I would lend them the key any time they needed it, so no curfew would be broken. Well, to their big disappointment I was not going along with that little plan. Especially a couple sluts were not pleased. Let's face it, I did not want to disappoint any one person, but this meant a whole new responsibility not to be taken lightly. The next evening, I reported to the bar and was immediately adorned with a cute white apron. The majority of patron's were British servicemen of ranks above a private, who enjoyed some conversations in English, one of the four fluent languages my Grandfather possessed. Only about a handful of close German regulars frequented the place, but Grandpa thought this would help me to get some introduction to the English language. Wrong, the only earsplitting sound I heard regularly was emanating from the juke box and made no sense whatever. All I heard was quack... quack.... quack, that turned out to be a well-known English song called "rock around the clock" I learned some days later. I was not accustomed to that kind of music since it was forbidden in the East, for that reason I felt this to be a total culture shock. It did not escape my Grandpa's observations that my apron strings did not remain in a pretty bow for more than five minutes at the most. Those handsome servicemen, if that is what you could say about the Britt's, just wanted to show attention to me, much to my dear Grandpa's dismay. I got promoted to be behind the bar and become proficient in the fine art of filling beer glasses from draft without too much foam on top. The bartender was furious as he had to bring trays of beer and shots to the mingling masses, I'm sure he silently hated me. One thing was clear to me at the start, the Britt's could not handle the German beer, and coupled with a shot of hard whiskey, or Schnapps, they were soon drunk. At least I did not have to work at the bar on the one day a week that was a school day, for which I had to take the train for a mere one-hour ride to Hamburg. I loved that city and usually walked to the harbor after school, where the seagulls would swoop down to snatch bits of my lunch sandwich, I reserved for them from my outstretched hand. The harbor held an almost magical fascination for me. The constant movement of large and small boats, plus the ever-present tugboats made me yearn for an ocean voyage.

The final exams went well at the school in Hamburg, the practical test on the drawing board was held at a different firm in Lüneburg, and once again I was the only female awaiting the test. The huge room had about twenty drawing boards equally spaced in several rows, but in the center of that room was a glass enclosed cubicle that was someone's office. It contained just one drawing board and a desk with chair. This was to be my test station, which made me feel like I was on display in a fish bowl, visible from all sides. While three shirts sleeved but stern looking inspectors circulated among the male students and seemed to ignore me, I just started to concentrate on my task. Easier said than done, since I had to work with several individual part drawings and build them into a single assembly that was to resemble a bigger machine. To my horror I got stuck about two thirds into the assembly drawing and nothing further seemed to fit together. My biting my lower lip and looking worried was noticed by one of the inspectors, who entered my glass cage. I swear I could see his little mental wheels turning while thinking that this girl is not up to the task and cannot complete the test. I watched him take a long look at my test problem, then he called the other two to have a look. They agreed that the engineer's calculations were a bit off, had it corrected, and I was able to finish my test in the allotted time, although I was the last person to leave the building. Hoping to never ever again have to experience such nerve-wracking situations I was overjoyed at the news that I passed. Word of my satisfactory test results reached the vice president of the pump factory, who contacted my immediate boss with the suggestion to have a fully catered graduation party to be held in the cafeteria in my honor, the first female. To say I was pleased with myself would be an understatement, but to my surprise the V.P. showed up at the party and presented me with a beautiful Mont Blank fountain pen set in a leather case with the words "he hoped I would have a long-standing working relationship with the company". I liked the sound of that but knew at this point that I had different plans.

After having joined Opa and Grand mama for a lovely Sunday dinner it was time to get on my bike and peddle back to the girl's home. As I was about to ride away, I took a quick look up at the second-floor window and saw Opa waving good bye. I thought it strange, for he had never done so before. It seemed odd and somewhat out of the norm, therefore I lingered just a few more seconds before taking off. I dismissed the strange feeling and went on my merry way. Monday morning started with my immediate boss being called to the office of the big boss, then the engineer, followed by the senior draftsman. I was expecting to be called on next to be informed about some work-related news. Nothing. Finally, everyone gathered around my drawing board and gave me, as gently as they could, the news of my Opa's death. I loved that man; he was my rock. I was told to carefully go to grandmother and be of help to her. On my arrival she hugged me with her tearful face on my shoulder. Every five minutes she had me place a small hand mirror to his mouth and nose, to make sure he was no longer breathing. At the same time, I was to touch his neck to check for a possible pulse, of course there was none, but I was curious about the fact how long it took for the body to start to cool. The funeral was a simple service with the entire department of my workplace in attendance. I wore a black armband on my left sleeve of my trench coat for the better part of a year. Being no longer a student and apprentice, I had to adhere to the rules of the girl's home and find other lodging. As it happened, a good friend from the home was also leaving after finishing her secretarial schooling, so we decided to hunt for a place to share. We did find a Cape Cod style house with one of the upper floor bedrooms, as well as a small dressing room that contained a sink. A bathroom was nearby. After a brief interview with the middle aged couple, we got the place and moved in immediately. My friend Wendie's parents lived in a very small town, only a little less than an hour train ride away, therefore she would go home on the weekends. This would leave me to my rather busy social activities, but sometimes I just wanted some time to myself. I always had to notify our landlord when I wanted to take a bath. He would then light the gas flame under the water heater and inform me when it was hot enough. Lucky Wendie took her baths at her patent's place. On one such day I was ready to step into the tub when I heard a knock on the door. He had left his glasses on the window sill and wanted them right away. I saw through that excuse right away and yelled through the door that I was not dressed to let him in, he would have to get his glasses later. That little gnome had the nerve to say he wanted to see me as a bathing beauty, in other words naked. That is when I remembered his wife was out of town visiting with their married daughter. It never fails to amaze me what a man will stoop to for some extra marital amusement, and this sleazeball was no exception. For my own piece of mind, I stuffed cotton into the keyhole. Upon Wendie's return I told her the whole story at which time she decided to go home every other weekend. When she did go home, she insisted that I was to accompany her, to which her parents agreed.

On one of an 'at home' weekend I decided to go for a bike ride out of town and explore the country side. As I passed a small hamlet I saw a young girl sitting in a wheelchair on the front lawn of a house and in passing I waved and shouted "Hi." This must have taken her by surprise, because I did not see her react. On my way back, a while later, I noticed she wore a big smile and waved back. I felt a bit sorry for her in that rickety old wooden chair, so I decided to stop and just have a little chat with her. She appeared to be my age, so we could have something to talk about. As soon as I stopped and leaned my bike against their fence an older man stepped out of the house and inquired if I was lost. Not really, I just wanted to stop for a while was my explanation. That is how I met Hildie, who was not my age at all and has been in a wheelchair all her life due to MS or something like it. In fact, she was thirty years old to my eighteen, no wonder her parents looked so old, but that did not stop me from visiting her on a somewhat regular basis. We would chat a little and she would get so excited that she could hardly control her hands, which were bent downward at the wrist, and would flail depending on how excited she got. Speaking was difficult for her as well, finally getting some words out would send her hands really flying through the air. At those times, and they were often, I would just laugh and remind her to calm down and at the same time feel happy to be healthy, even with my troublesome back. Her parents were happy she had someone to talk with, and she wanted to know all the things I had done between my visits. One time I told her about a movie I had seen and realized by her big eyes and shiny face that she had never been to see a movie. I got the bright idea to take her but wondered at the same time as to how I was going to get her into the city and the movie theater.

They had no car and I had just my bike, but such trivial things never did stop me from doing what I set out to do. Her parents looked at me in disbelief but decided to trust me. On the prearranged day I rode my bike out of the city and became aware, for the first time, of the condition of the packed dirt road leading to Hildie's place. That road was inter woven with various tree roots which never bothered me before, but the thought of me pushing her in that antiquated chair, getting possibly hung up on those roots, all the way into the center of the city, gave me pause. Well, I had promised this and felt I had to keep my word. Disappointing her was just not an option. Armed with good intentions and a flash light for our return in total darkness, we took off. I cannot recall the film we saw, but we giggled a lot on the way home, stopping every now and then to catch my breath, and trying to figure out what made the strange noises we heard every so often. It was most likely a creature in the forest whose sleep we disturbed. Most important was the fact that we made it back safely. I am absolutely sure Hildie never forgot our adventure and her very first, most likely also last, movie she had ever seen. I must say that I felt rather pleased for having taken the time and made the effort to do something out of the ordinary for someone who would not have been able to do so for themselves. After Wendie returned from her regular visit with her parents, I told her all about my latest activity, while she shook her head every now and then, as if in disbelief. By now she knew me well enough to take everything I said as fact.

On the next weekend she stayed in the city we decided to rent a kayak and have some fun on the river Lune. Neither one of us had a clue or any experience, so I took the initiative to sit in the back seat of the two-seater and steer with the foot pedals, which were attached to the little rudder by either wire or some string. Call it talent or just plain luck, but I maneuvered the sleek vessel like a pro around the many bends upstream. I loved being on the water and felt like I was in my element. I'm certain we paddled more than a mile in mostly unison strokes, when Wendie wanted to trade places with me and do the steering on the return part. While holding on to the tall grass at the river bank we did the switch with great care to avoid tipping over and started merrily downstream with the flow when I noticed she was drifting a bit too far to the middle of the river. As we were coming to a bend in the river, I heard a voice giving rhythmic commands and told my friend to steer to the right. I guessed a racing shell was approaching and we seemed to be on a collision course. Sure enough, a four-man crew was rowing and a fifth gave the tempo. I suppose dear Wendie got a bit flustered and we were headed directly toward the flimsy craft. In just seconds we made contact and actually inflicted a small hole at the water line, but it was big enough for me to see it was starting to sink and hear the men's voices calling us many names. All we could think of was to get out of there real fast, return the kayak immediately and hide out at home. We never dallied together on the river again.

Ever since an injury to my back while doing gymnastics in the East I was ordered to do swimming as part of my therapy. The swimming coach at the pool in my home town had to accept me to work out with the team, after all, it was on doctor's orders. This was all good and well then, but now in the West I had not pursued any doctor sanctioned action toward my health. To do some good for my back I had started my own regimen in the form of a daily swim in the river after each work day soon after I got the job. If a swim at an indoor pool was prescribed, then the river should do as well, since I had not located a pool as yet. The routine was to ride my bike about a couple miles upstream and away from the city, where I hoped the water would be clean and clear of any pollutants. I found a suitably big enough bush under which to stash the bike and my clothing, as well as a towel. Next, I jumped into the river and swam with the current about a mile, after which I had to climb out and run or jog, depending on how cold it was on that day, back to the bush, and try to hurriedly dress. This was actually enjoyable during the warmer months, but as October arrived the water was much colder, so much so that my skin felt a burning sensation as I plunged into the river. I stuck to that ritual until just past the middle of October and felt very healthy.

By now I had already made a couple trips to Hamburg and visited the American consulate for the sole purpose of possible immigration to the United States. Mother's youngest sister, Tante Lotte (short for Aunt Charlotte), was married over ten years, living in New York without having had any children, but unfortunately she had had three miscarriages. Her husband, my American uncle, always wanted children desperately. I'm not sure she was in sync with him on that topic, but I had been in touch with her as she promised to sponsor me to join them the last time, I saw her at my tender age of fifteen. But only after all my schooling was completed and had a successful departure from the East, a demand not to be ignored. She did not want the responsibility of a minor living with her. At the consulate I had to undergo some intensive questioning, as well as physical examinations of an invasive kind. Having blood drawn was always a most stressful experience that most unwanted, and in my mind barbaric practice always ended with me fainting as soon as I saw the needle, but for certain as the needle entered my vein. At this point Grand mama knew my leaving Germany was a reality, therefore she felt it necessary to give me some sage advice to be followed to the letter. As she had me do since my arrival at her place, I was to continue washing my chest every morning with cold water to keep my breasts firm and perky. The fact that I did not have any noticeable breasts did not bother her at all, I did not even own a bra yet. I was also advised after getting married and having a child I was to instruct the nurse to place a stack of folded sheets on my stomach to have the uterus return to its original position. Sounded good to me, so I promised. Furthermore, I was under no circumstances to breast feed the child, this would ruin my breasts for sure. Okay with me on that point too. I was to hire a wet nurse to feed the baby. So far so good, as all this was not planned in my immediate future.

At this point I actually had my first boyfriend named Werner, a very good looking blonde young man, who played Foosball (soccer), as well as the trumpet. His Mom was enthused over his choice of a girlfriend, but he also had an older as well as a younger brother, both of which tried for my attention when Werner was not around. I was just not interested in them. This little romance did not last long, because every time Werner tried for more than just some hot kisses, I could hear Mother's voice in my mind yelling not to dare come home pregnant. Before long I met my true love, my handsome dark haired and blue-eyed Leo. I was totally smitten and it appeared he felt likewise for me. To his credit was the fact that he never pressured me into any unwanted activity of a sexual kind. He worked in the factory of the same company as I and looked real sharp commuting quite a few miles away from the city on his blue moped to and from the same area where dear Hildie lived. It got more interesting when his boss saw in him the potential of being more than just a factory worker and recommended him for a position in the office at a drawing board. Even as a factory worker it was suggested he should take courses in drafting, which qualified him for a better position. He wound up right next to my board and we passed some notes back and forth, so as not to look too eager. We made a date to go see a movie on a certain day and at a precise time. He told me not to be more than five minutes late or he would be gone. He drove the point home by stating that he was not in the habit of waiting around for anyone. Well, I thought, isn't that a fine start. My mother bossed me around enough and I was not going to take this from someone I really cared for. My plan was to be a little late, just to assert my independence. But it had started to rain, and after hunting for my umbrella I was just about ten minutes late. I did wonder how to react if he was actually not there when I arrived, but the handsome darling was a bit wet, but still waiting, so I greeted him with a nice kiss. That is when I noticed the box of chocolates, he had gotten for me and felt almost compelled to wrap my arms around him for being an absolutely adorable gentleman. Many more dates followed, and it became urgent to inform him about my future plans. I noticed the shock of this news on his face and realized for the first time that he really loved me. I was deeply in love with him as well, but the thought of possible opportunities and new adventures was a powerful draw not to be ignored.

After my third and final trip to Hamburg and the consulate, there was just no turning back. All the paper work had been completed by either my Uncle or Aunt Lotte, the trip across the Atlantic Ocean was set for the 31st of October 1956 on the ship called the MS BERLIN, the sister ship of the ITALIA. It was time to start composing a rather smartly tailored letter of resignation to the Loewe Pump Company, which I did with a heavy heart. To my surprise there was a big farewell party for me, along with a promise of getting rehired in the event I did not like or hated any part of my future expectation. The day before my scheduled departure Leo and I got together for the last time and made a pact. He said that he would wait for one entire year for my return, at which time we would get engaged and later marry. This thought never occurred to me, thou I loved him with all my heart. I did agree to that plan and inwardly hoped I would not like living in the New World for more than a year. We kissed and held each other very tight for a long time.

Meanwhile my mother had received the permission needed to come to the West to see her daughter off to America, my two brothers had to stay behind. She was actually more interested in shopping for pretty clothes for herself than spending some time with me. As I was about to purchase a one-way ticket to the port city for me and a round trip ticket for her, she stopped me in mid purchase. I was rather shocked when she mentioned something about saying good bye here, instead of at the ship, would be just as good, and the money would be better spent if she bought something for herself by which to remember me, are still reverberating in my brain. Dopey! I actually gave her the money! What was I thinking? I guess she had properly brainwashed me, plus I did not want to cause a scene in public. Much later I found out that she never even went back to Goerlitz and her sons, instead she instructed Karl-Heinz to sell the furniture from the fifth-floor apartment and send her the money. No thought about where her son would live entered her mind.

The day of my departure on the MS Berlin was a mild and sunny day, the dock was filled with mingling masses, I guess every person on board had someone to wave and shout good bye to, except me. I felt at once excited and a bit melancholy, the latter was especially strong when a brass band started to play a sad farewell song. After wiping just a couple tears away I started to vigorously wave my white hanky to no one in particular. The loosened heavy ropes released the big vessel, dropped into the water and the dock workers hauled them back onto dry land. Then the ship moved ever so slowly away. It was time to check who would be sharing the cabin with me. While stowing my little green and white speckled suitcase right after boarding the two bunk beds on opposite walls did not escape my attention, so I assumed we would be four young people. I was never good at guessing people's age; therefore I was surprised one cabin mate was my age, but the other two ladies were at the very least in their forties. The absence of a window, or a port hole, gave that tight cabin a slight feeling of a cave. I decided to spend as little time as possible in the cabin but hoped there would be a friendly aura in this tight space. There was limited storage space for our belongings, and after I got situated with my few items, I went back on deck to watch our progress. It did not take long to reach the English Channel and actually see the white cliffs of Dover. The sea was relatively calm until we entered the Atlantic Ocean. Soon it got a bit choppy and I heard some snippets of a hearty conversation by a small group of passengers, who were making comments about the crossing of the ocean in November. They agreed that this was not the best time of the year to do so. Should I be worried by what I heard? Nonsense, I welcomed a little adventure at sea, besides how bad could it get.

This voyage was to take five days with our first stop in Halifax, Nova Scotia, and then on to New York. Every day was a surprise as far as the weather was concerned. One day we would have a beautifully sunny day with calm seas, followed by a stormy ocean and hail the size of golf balls. One day the fog was so thick I literally could not see my own hand in front of my face. I heard that expression before, but never believed it could happen. It actually did and passengers were advised not to go out on deck. As it happened many travelers got seasick and had to go outside for some fresh air. For that purpose, the crew fastened ropes from the doors to the railings for passengers to hold on to, as the ocean had become increasingly rougher. The waves got bigger, and the dining room got emptier with each passing day, but my appetite grew allegedly from all that sea air. I even signed up for the daily tour of the kitchen, where the staff got to notice me and handed me a little snack each time. Never having owned a camera I asked the ships photographer to take a few pictures for me. While standing at the railing a huge monster of a wave got closer and closer to the ship. It looked as tall as a three- or four-story building and scared me enough to run up the nearest metal stairs towards the next higher deck. As I turned to see if the photographer was close behind me, I saw him laughing at my panic, and still standing at the railing. He assured me we were not getting wet, but instead the ship would simply ride up on that wave and then slide down on the other side, as if surfing. I had never heard of surfing before but found this part of sailing very exciting and enjoyable. At least I had proof of such a high wave in the great picture and one more, as a wave splashed over the entire bow of the ship. The days were filled with varying activities, such as shuffle board and ping pong. I even got to go into the pool, which was on the lowest deck the passengers were allowed. While enjoying a good swim in the pool the sea was once again showing some anger. I admired the beautiful wood paneling and murals on the walls and was suddenly swept from the shallow end to the deep in one swift motion, barely missing the one meter diving board. The life guard immediately ordered me out of the water, as this was getting more dangerous by the moment. So much for a leisurely swim. The evenings were usually enjoyed while dancing to the music of a specific theme, such as a Bavarian bier garden, or singing some very old sea shanties to which only the older passengers knew the words.

In the dining room I shared a table with one girl and two boys, who were about the same age as myself, as well as an elderly couple. We had some lively conversations, mostly about where we came from and why we are going to America, until one evening, when some soup plates slid off the tables and made a mess on the nice carpeting. The stewards placed weighted wooden rings at every place setting that kept the plates from sliding away. Eating the soup got a bit tricky too. As soon as you got the loaded spoon to your mouth the soup had run off. This made for some embarrassed giggles and we moved on to the solid main meal. The weather deteriorated by the hour. On my way back to the cabin I got a bit tossed from one side of the hallway to the other, and I expected some bruising was going to be visible the next day. The steward had turned down the bed over which I had some mixed feelings. No one at home had ever turned down my bed, add to this the fact that a man was doing this for me, but I got used to this kind of being pampered real fast. I was just about ready to drift off to sleep when the cabin steward entered the room again and mentioned to the four of us that we might be in for a little rough weather during the night. For our safety we had to be strapped in with an about two to three inches wide leather belt, that was looped through a U-shaped metal piece and attached to the wall. This might get a little exciting I thought to myself, as the steward calmed the couple across from me, who were showing anxiety on their faces. Well, he was not kidding. Being a very sound sleeper, I awoke to my almost doing a head stand in my bed, and just moments later I was nearly standing up straight. This was repeated several more times, accompanied by rolling sideways as well. Had I not been strapped in I would surely have been tossed from my upper bunk. This went on for the better part of the rest of the night and became the only topic of the conversation over breakfast, which was now attended by way fewer passengers than before. My appetite, however, was still increasing and it did not escape my attention that my clothing was getting just a tad tight around the midsection.

Our planned arrival in Halifax never happened, instead the daily posted route had us go directly into New York. Having lost a few days at sea due to nasty weather, we sailed into New York harbor in the middle of the night from November ninth to the tenth. Having never heard anything about the Statue of Liberty and what it meant to America, I did not mind at all not catching a glimpse of her, instead I enjoyed a last good night's sleep on board. Our table steward had taken an extra fatherly interest in me and fattened me up, yes I gained roughly ten pounds in nine days. Those daily trips through the kitchen did not help at all. He seemed a little concerned about my arrival in New York and into the household of people I hardly knew. Before leaving the ship, he gave me a sheet of paper with his name and telephone number on it. He wanted me to get in touch with him in case I did not like the circumstances after my arrival, assuring me he would get me back to Germany if I so desired. I found his concern very touching and kept that piece of paper for some time.

Getting off the ship and into the enormous arrival hall at the pier was a shocking and lasting experience. The very first thing that hit every fiber of my senses was the unbelievably dirty condition of that place. Several small glass panes of the huge windows were broken, the rest had not seen a good cleaning in years. To top it off were the many cigarette butts, gum and candy wrappers that littered the floor. At this point I was ready to turn around and run back onto the ship, when I spotted someone who looked like my aunt Lotte, short for Charlotte. I remained in that position for quite a while and wondered if she was going to approach me, or should I make that move. Then I noticed another, and a bit taller, lady standing next to my aunt. The two were discussing something, then the other lady came directly to where I was standing and asked if I am Christa. I was barely answering a hushed yes to her question when she threw her arms around me and welcomed me to America with a wonderful hug. Next, she walked me over to my aunt, who muttered that we have to hurry because Benny (her husband and my uncle) was double parked. Where, the blooming heck, was the warm welcome from her? We grabbed my little suitcase and ran outside to a noisy concert of car horns, my aunt ripped open a car door and we three piled in. The door was barely shut and we sped off through a jumble of cars, until we reached an avenue with orderly moving lanes of all kinds of vehicles. All this time I had my head half way out of the open window and tried taking in the awesomeness of all those tall buildings. I had finally seen a multitude of proper sky scrapers I had heard so much about. The view from the car was breathtaking and I could not get enough of it. Then my aunt turned to me and held my face with one hand, while with the other she expertly applied some awful tasting lipstick, the taste of which lingered longer in my brain than on my lips. After a fast ride along avenues and some side streets we passed over a steel bridge, and some minutes later stopped in front of a church. For a moment I feared that dear auntie had turned into a holy roller, but it turned out that uncle's niece was getting married on that sunny Saturday. By now it dawned on me why we were in such an awful hurry, and why I never got to say a proper hello to Uncle Benny or was even introduced to him. All of that great rushing around was because the ship and I were a few days late, but we made it just in time to witness the bride and groom make the vows to each other. After church we drove to aunt and uncle's house in the section of the city called Queens. They lived on the second floor of a two-family home in the Woodside section of Queens, with uncle's brother and his wife on the ground floor. My aunt had laid out a pretty black dress with a white satin collar and a pair of shoes for me to wear to the reception of the newlyweds. I dare say the dress was just a little bit tight to my liking, but aunt said I looked great, which was confirmed by the photos taken at the event. I dare say the shoes were definitely too small. I wore a size seven, but the shoes were a six and one half. I squeezed into those toe killers and hoped I would mostly sit through the reception. Wrong, word went around that I had just gotten off the boat from Germany. I really think that every one of the two hundred and fifty invited guests came to great me with hugs and a kiss on the cheek. I was stunned and convinced that every one of them was queer. You just did not kiss a stranger, never mind a crowd. The norm for me was a polite hand shake with people I just met. Oh my goodness, I thought, what did I just get in to, and my aunt and uncle were part of all this craziness. Oh well, I just had to make the best of this, I promised myself, as the music started to play, and the dance floor filled almost instantly with people intend on having fun.

Just because I came from Europe everyone concluded that I must be quite adept at dancing the waltz and the polka, and they were actually right. I suspected that the older men requested those dances to be played quite frequently, possibly because their wives did not know how or were not able to master these dances. Did I think I was going to relax and remain in my seat, think again? I had just finished a waltz with one older gentleman, when I got handed off to the next one, who twirled me to the music of a very lively polka. My feet were killing me at first, but by about a half dozen dances later I felt nothing from my ankles down. I knew that taking my shoes off would be a big mistake, so I did opt for keeping them on, and sure as hell, suffer the consequences later. At one point during the festivities, I was introduced to two brothers, who were of German parents and had a good command of the language. I was pleased to have been able to talk with someone other than my aunt, because at this point I was not yet able to speak English at all, and no one had a clue about my second language, namely Russian. One of the brothers informed me about his job at a watch company, where all work was done by the metric system. He promised to see about getting me an interview with the head of the drafting and engineering department. I knew before long I would have to get a job and pay for my stay at my aunt's place. Having been educated in the metric system made me feel at ease at the prospect of a possible job at a watch company. Just the thought of dealing with inches and all those creepy fractions gave me an uneasy feeling about my future.

On this evening, I had my first drink that contained hard liquor and was called seven and seven. It did not taste completely awful, but I kept it at one drink only. The party finally broke up at almost five o'clock in the morning, Uncle Benny was driving in spite of being somewhat tipsy. His brother was in no better shape, and his wife was crying in the back seat as my uncle just missed rear ending an early morning garbage truck. I was sitting between the ladies in the back, so my aunt instructed me to calm her sister-in-law down, totally forgetting I did not speak a word of English besides the word 'hello.' All I could think of was that I would most likely die on this very first day in America. Well, we made it home in one piece, got ready for bed, which for me was a Hollywood couch located in the dining area. I was re-living my first day in the U.S. before falling into a deep sleep.

The next morning felt a little awkward, because I was unable to talk with my uncle, therefore my aunt had to translate what little was said. The next few weeks, while uncle and aunt were at work, she told me what was expected of me. I got busy dusting, doing the dishes and peeling a lot of potatoes for the evening meals. We did the vacuuming together on Saturday's, at which time the couch cushions were cleaned separately. By now I was convinced my dear aunt was a clean freak, because my Mother never put that much emphasis on cleaning. Heck, we did not even own a carpet, never mind a vacuum cleaner. I learned a lot from my aunt, even some cooking skills. Not having had enough food in the East to experiment with, I was only able to cook potatoes and eggs. To fry a whole pork chop or a cutlet was definitely not in my repertoire. After having been allowed to make myself useful for one whole month at my aunt's place I got the good news that an appointment for an interview at the watch company was scheduled. My excitement level was high as I took special care to put my portfolio together and making sure I was not leaving anything to chance. It was quite a long walk from our residence in Woodside to the watch company located in Jackson Heights, but with the written instructions I got there on time. The first part of the interview was a test on how fast I could assemble about two dozen nuts and bolts, place them into each hole of a board and then take them apart again. I was truly shocked at this. Did they think I was going to work on an assembly line? Oh no, not me, but then someone cleared up the confusion and I got to meet the head of the engineering department. He was a lovely older man, a bit portly, with a full head of silver grey hair and he was a German. He studied my portfolio, looked at me over his silver framed glasses, and after just a few questions hired me on the spot. What a relief. I walked back home with a much lighter step and could hardly wait to tell this good news to my aunt, who then translated every little thing I said to her husband, my Uncle.

My excitement was great over the fact that I was starting a new job in spite of the fact that I did not speak any English. I was assigned a German lady who was only a few years older than myself and working in the factory. She was taken off the assembly line and became my interpreter. I was doubly exhilarated not having to deal with fractions of an inch, the metric system was my thing. At the same time, I started my job I was also enrolled at the local high school's evening classes to learn English. Things could not possibly get any better, except for the very openly displeased comments made by the supervisor of the engineering department for my not being able to speak French. I did hear, and understand, some snippets of his outbursts to one of his coworkers and made a mental note to tell him off the moment I was able to do so. It was the middle of December, but school classes had started in September, which meant I was quite a bit behind the rest of the class. Years ago, when I was forced to learn Russian, I had discovered that I liked foreign languages and found learning English was a lot easier. The fact that we had an excellent teacher is still evident in my pronouncing many words, that other students from several foreign countries had difficulty with. He was so pleased with my progress, after only three months in first class I was promoted to second class, of course I too was very proud of my accomplishment thus far. I settled into a usual routine of working five days, and evening classes on three nights a week, when after seven months everything came to a screeching halt. The economy had taken a downward turn and I got laid off from work. I thought 'layoff' was just another word for being fired. My work was deemed better than just good, so why did I get fired? I cried all the way home that hot July day and was a little afraid about how Uncle Benny and Aunt Lotte would react to that news. By the way, at this point I was able to have many conversations with my uncle. He actually had a very burning question for me, one that had been bothering him for many years and only I could give him an honest answer: who is Lothar, is he Lotte's son or my brother. A question that needed to be answered at this point. When Uncle was stationed in Bavaria at the end of the last war and dating my aunt, he had met my brother when he was just a one year old cute baby, suffering from dysentery and dehydration after my mother had dropped him off at my Aunt's. The baby called her Mommy, so Benny naturally assumed my brother was my aunt's kid and she just left him behind when he brought her to the States. So, after only about three months of lessons I had just enough knowledge of the English language to finally set the record straight. At last uncle Benny believed me that the kid was my youngest brother, case closed.

Now the hunt for another job began with a visit to the employment agency. It was truly slim pickings at this time, nothing at all available in my field of expertise, therefore I felt compelled to grab anything available so I could continue paying my aunt the fifteen dollars per week she had gotten used to. The only job immediately available was that of a nanny, and she had to be a 'live in.' I went to the residence in a bit of an upscale neighborhood for the interview and got the position on the spot. My duties were primarily as the nanny and some light housekeeping. I took the job and moved into their lovely three-bedroom apartment. The husband had his own import business, the wife played mahjong on a regular basis and their son was a bed wetter. He was also the most spoiled seven-year-old brat I ever came across. After wetting his bed on a nightly basis, he would come crawling into bed with me, and I had the delightful task of chasing him right back into his room. His other endearing habit was to hide either my wallet or my car keys on my days off. I know that I was the only person who paid attention to him, but I was only twenty years of age and had a life of my own, or so I thought. His mother told me she does all the cooking, all I have to do is the dishes. She forgot to mention that she would use just about every pot and pan at her disposal and leave the kitchen in the worst messy state I had ever seen. On the first night, while she cooked, I had to set the dinner table, which I did for four people. After a quick glance at my work, she told me they were not having any company, so the table needed to be set for three only, and I was to eat in the kitchen after they were done. Damn, I thought, I became a slave in just one short hour or less. I wanted to quit at that very moment, but I just could not go back to my aunt and uncle. She had become pregnant just three months after my arrival to the States, and there was just no more room for me at their place on that evening, or any other time. After my tormentor was done cooking, the kitchen looked like a tornado hit the place. Yes, she did use just about every pot, frying pan and many other items she owned, and dusted the place liberally with flour. I was up by seven every morning and was never done before eight at night, yes, I came just about as close to being a slave as one possibly could. One day she asked me to stop going to my evening classes for English, instead she wanted me to teach the German language to her kid. My answer was an emphatic NO. I was completely immersed in my classes; this was of the utmost importance to me. She also did not like me to park my car anywhere in front of the apartment building. My nineteen forty-six Dodge fluid drive (where was that fluid anyway) had a few dings and dents and was just not elegant enough for that neighborhood, so I was told to park it on a side street and out of sight. The daily trips to the basement laundry room had prompted the other domestic help to make comments such as "you are still here" and "that families help never stays long, it's like a revolving door." Now I could see why, this was not going to be a permanent position for me either. One day, after the brat tossed a heavy brass statue of a Buddha at my head, but luckily, I ducked, it hit the door to my room and left a huge dent in that solid wood. That was the last straw. So, after working for that family a whole five months I marched myself back to the employment office and got an address for an interview in down town Manhattan.

I was not entirely clear about for what position I was going to interview, but what the heck, I needed a job. The subway ride, during which some pervert grabbed my butt, took me all the way to the last stop in Manhattan, namely just about a block away from the corner of Canal and Bowery streets. This was known as the diamond district of the city and sure enough, I was interviewing for the position of bookkeeper for a diamond setter. Are they kidding me? I learned that training for a job in a school setting, and the idea of apprenticeships were not a usual way of approaching a career in this country. I had no clue what was involved, but my-boss-to-be, a very nice man named Frank, assured me I was the best prospect the agency had sent them, and I was hired. At the same time, I rented a furnished room in the single-family home belonging to a nice, older lady in a lovely neighborhood. It was conveniently located near a subway station, that way I did not have to take the car into the city, for which I only had a driving permit, but not yet a license. At the end of each workday, I would walk to the subway and noticed a young black man, who worked in the same building as I, walked to the subway as well. We started a cordial conversation on the way and continued right into the same subway car, while holding on to the metal pole. I glanced around for a possibly available seat, but instead was the recipient of a couple disapproving glances, which I gathered were for talking to a black person. So that is how it is here I thought to myself. The very first time I ever saw a black person happened when I was fifteen years old and still living in the East of Germany. That young man was with a visiting communist delegation, and I observed how a couple German ladies walked right up to him and touched his skin, just to see if the color would come off. At the time I felt this was rather forward, yet somewhat adventurous of them. Anyway, this bookkeeping job entailed carrying many high valued pieces of jewelry in a specific black leather purse to be steam cleaned or just polished at a place across the street. The purchase of sheets of gold took me a couple blocks farther, and I wondered what would happen if I was ever robbed. That thought was a bit scary to me, because the Bowery Street was known for a rather visible population of bums, alcoholics and homeless people. I voiced this concern to my boss right after a drunken man draped his arms over my shoulders from behind, while I was carrying almost a million dollars' worth of lose diamonds. Just about a second later the bum was peeled off of me by two bystanders. Frank assured me that not only the jewelry, but I too was insured for a sizable sum, plus the fact that under cover security men were there, but invisible to the public. That sounded good to me, but I was glad that after working down town for five months I received a telegram from my former boss at the watch company, they wanted me back. I was just elated. This meant no more icky subway rides, no more bums or drunkards to deal with. Plus, I became aware how often the number five played a role in my life. If I'm ever going to play the lottery, I will have to include that magical number.

No more rides on the subway meant my tank of a car would be playing a primary role in my life from now on. I had asked Uncle Benny to teach me to drive, but he declined at first, citing a bad experience with aunt's girlfriend Erika. He did take me out once to a rather wide street in a quiet residential neighborhood, but when he asked me to make a U-turn it turned into a three sixty instead. I had very little control of that tank of a car. Uncle weighed every bit of 250 lbs., and the driver's seat reflected that with a rather deep dent. Therefore, I was looking through the steering wheel instead of over it. There was no power steering either, so I really had to struggle hard to turn the wheel to make any kind of turns. Anyway, that was the end of more lessons with him, instead I signed up with a proper driving school and had a wonderful teacher named Mr. Murphy. The lessons were scheduled for Saturday mornings, but the first time Mr. Murphy got just one look at my car, he decided we are doing the lessons in his wonderfully newer push button vehicle. I was very pleased with his decision, at least I got to drive a lovely modern car. The next six Saturday mornings went as follows: He would honk the horn at ten o'clock sharp, at which point I hastily rolled out of bed and threw something on while brushing my teeth in record time. By the disarray of my hair, he knew I had not been up for hours, so he would suggest that I drive to the nearby diner and we'd have some breakfast. I drove and loved that routine, and after we ate, he had me drive around for about a half hour or so to practice some usual maneuvers. This seemed easy as pie, so after six actual lessons, that always included breakfast at the diner, he suggested I was ready to do the road test. The appointment was set and on that specific day, a Monday morning, we drove into Manhattan to the test site. To say that I was just a little concerned about doing my test in the world's busiest city during rush hour traffic, while a heavy rain pelted the wind shield, would have been a huge understatement. The inspector got into the front passenger seat and directed me to make a left turn at the next corner. I guess I did not shoot fast enough into the left lane, therefore he just about barked that command at me again. I dutifully turned the left indicator on, but just to be sure, I also opened the window and gave the proper hand signal. I was not risking a chance to leave even a tiny detail out. To perform a broken U-turn on a street with delivery trucks double parked is no easy feat but thank goodness I kept my cool. I was also completely unaware of the fact that the spot where I was ordered to park at the curb was occupied by a fire hydrant at the edge of the sidewalk. The view of that object was completely obstructed by the high fin of the right rear fender of the car. About a week later I received confirmation that I passed the test, much to my Uncle's surprise.

Here comes that nice flight attendant again with my dinner tray and a friendly smile. We know each other because we are colleges, working for the very same airline, but more about that later. In the meantime, it got dark outside the little window, with nothing to look at but the stars. It is time to busy myself with reading or a movie, perhaps just thinking some more about the meeting with my two brothers, my sister-in-law and our planned road trip in two days. I just hope the younger brother, who is going to do all the driving, has taken the necessary steps and kept his Honda in good shape. We have decided to visit the places we had evacuated to during the war, which was probably the best part of my childhood. I could hardly wait to see the old hunting cabin, the two farm houses nearby and most of all the fresh water spring and the brook running past the cabin and into the distance forever. One thing is for sure, I have never been able to sleep on a plane, no matter how long the flight is, even in first or business class. Instead, I try to picture in my mind the places we lived at in the wilds of lower Bavaria so many years ago, first the hay and straw filled attic under a bullet hole riddled roof of the old lady's house, and after that the wooden hunting cottage, already inhabited by mice and lots of bed bugs. The most memorable thing about that cottage were the many nightly hunts for those pests with long darning needles and a candle. I am itching all over just at the thought of having dealt with those pests. I am also excited about meeting the best, and most likely only friends of my brother's, who were kind enough to invite me to stay at their home for the duration of my stay in Hamburg, Germany, before the road trip. I sure as heck was not going to stay at my Mother's apartment, remembering the full-blown disaster the last time I visited her.

After just about two and a half years in the U.S. I felt just a little bit of home sickness. I had counted on Mother having just a little mellowed, therefore I decided to go for a visit. This sounded great at the time, especially since I had no other plans to spend my two weeks' vacation. At the time Mother did not yet own her condo, instead lived in a studio apartment with two single beds. At least I had a place to sleep. I felt like "all that" wearing a white-on-white costume, consisting of a skirt and matching jacket, topped off by white gloves and a very stylish hat in black with veil and a white buckle in front above the narrow brim. My white luggage with navy accent and gold initials rounded out the look. Damn, I felt great. Brother Karl-Heinz came to visit for the day to spend some time with me, and that night we went to a night club for some fun, music and dancing. I was very happy to see him after two and a half years, and we decided to celebrate in style. I actually checked my hat with the hat check girl, which made me giggle for some reason. To look mature and worldly I had started to smoke a couple months earlier, but only on weekends and while out at a club. In essence all I did was just puff without ever inhaling the smoke, the aroma of which was most unpleasant to my nose, the taste was not any better. For that reason, I acquired a cigarette holder of a considerable length, which I stuck right through the veil at times when I was wearing a hat and decided to light up. A smart looking onyx and silver colored cigarette case with the lighter built right in rounded out the ensemble. The cigarette brand of my choice was named Astor, they had a gold mouthpiece and the paper was in an assortment of pastel colors. The pack contained only about eight cigs and cost two dollars, pretty steep for that time, namely the '50's.

The night club was dimly lit, the music was very inviting to dance. I was asked to dance by a black man, who first asked my brothers permission to do so. I was very impressed by his manners and he was pleased to be able to converse in English with me. I guessed he did not have much opportunity to do so, and I obliged. Later I danced with a local young man, who promised my Brother to see me home safely, as my brother was about to leave. We actually stayed until the club closed and daylight was ever so slowly coming up on the horizon. We got into his car and decided to take the short drive to the river, just a little upstream and outside of the city limits. The summer air was balmy even this early in the morning, so we decided to have a morning swim in the river. I disrobed behind a sizable bush and he did the same about twenty yards away, then we did a mad dash from our respectable distance and jumped right into the somewhat cold water. The current was not very strong at all, so we paddled around and towards each other when we spotted some horses grazing in the meadow next to the river. One look at each other with big grins and a nod toward the unsuspecting horses is all it took. We quickly scrambled ashore and each got a hold of a horse. There I was, bare as the day I was born and dripping wet, trying to ride a horse bareback. My experience with horses had been only riding with an English as well as a western style saddle, but never without anything between the horse and me. Well, "my" horse was not willing to participate in any early activity of any kind. As I pressed my bare heels into the animal's sides, which I know did not hurt him, he first reared up on his hind legs and I held on to his mane with all my might. I did not expect his next move, but he was not yet done with me. Next that beast went full blast onto his front hooves, his hind end went straight up and he, or was it she, launched me in a high arc, I completed a full turn in midair and landed on my belly. At the same time my chin hit the ground with great force, and I hoped none of my front teeth were missing. While trying to estimate the damage to my naked body I heard a man's angry voice yelling "what we were doing to his horses." My companion and I grabbed our clothes from under the bushes, ran straight into his car and took off in a mighty hurry. In just moments we had entered the city and came upon a traffic light, which of curse just had to be red at that moment. To make matters worse, an early commuter bus pulled up to our right, which gave the passengers a good glimpse of my nakedness. When your body is still somewhat wet your clothes do not slide on easily. It was a struggle, but I managed to make myself somewhat presentable, and bid my equally adventurous partner a hushed good bye. My great care at entering Mother's abode with just a minimum of noise, hoping not to wake her, took all of my concentration. I disrobed in silence, slipped into my baby doll night clothes, and as soon as my head touched the pillow I was out.

Suddenly I heard a major commotion, and it did take just a few slow moments to realize that she was having one of her temper outbursts. At first, I wondered what got her going so early in the morning and checked the clock. It was just eight in the morning, and it felt like I enjoyed only about three or five minutes of sleep. Sure enough, she was complaining about my still being in bed at eight, because she was used to having the beds made up by that time. Good grief I'm on vacation was what I wanted to shout. Her fury knows no limits, never did before, therefore I was not completely surprised after getting out of bed to see my clothes laying on the front lawn. Sure enough, the suitcase was empty and I was forced to go outside while still wearing my night clothes, to collect my belongings, fold everything neatly, and I took the time to repack my suitcase. This kind of madness was not going to be tolerated by me, nor spoil my expensive trip "home." Just the thought of not tolerating anything my mother did made me cringe. The slightest objection to her behavior voiced by me would surely have resulted in a brutal physical act on her part, using any object within her reach. At this point most people mellow a bit with time, I heard, did I really think this would happen to my mother as well? Yes I did, or at least I was hoping for this natural process of slowing down would have an effect on her as well, but no such luck. There had just not enough time passed since I left the first time, it was now time to leave once again. One of the neighbors was a very nice man, so I did not hesitate to ask for a ride to the train station. His good upbringing did not allow for any questioning about my sudden departure after just such a short time with my mother in Lüneburg. At the station I purchased a one-way ticket by way of Hamburg to Burghausen, the picturesque small city, located on a river that was the border between Germany and Austria, where I knew I could visit with my favorite aunt, Tante Brigitte. She was just about the total opposite of her sister, my mother. She was a very kind and warm hearted lady and expected my visit, just not so soon. To inform her of my intended arrival I sent a telegram, which was much cheaper than to call, besides she did not have a phone. Back in those days hardly any household had a phone, this luxury was only for businesses and the rich. Someone from the shop on the ground floor of her building would have delivered a message to her, but I thought it an inconvenience to have an employee of the shop run up to the third floor. This did not exactly count as an emergency to the average family, though to me it was as close to one as you could get.

Well, my dear Aunt received me with open arms and a great amount of compassion, along with some head shaking when I told her of the stress her sister put me through. We talked for a few hours until my eyes were beginning to slam shut, after all I had a rough day and traveled almost about a thousand miles. The next morning Aunt Brigitte greeted me with a delicious mimosa at bedside, something my mother would never have done, let alone serve me. This act of utter kindness was so strange to me, it just about brought me to tears. I stayed a few most happy days at her apartment, but the weather was beginning to turn nasty with lots of rain and rather unseasonably cool temperatures. So, I decided to take a trip further south, to mostly sunny Italy for only five days, in case the weather was not any better than where I was. I hoped that once I crossed over the impressive Alps the weather would be more to my liking. The cheapest and more interesting way to travel was by bus. I booked the trip with the local travel agency as an excursion, which connected me with a nice group of people of all ages and a very interesting itinerary. All overnight stays and some meals were included, as well as a couple visits to some noteworthy attractions. By now I was really excited about my very first trip to Italy, of which I had heard so much about. After packing my suitcase once again I said good bye to Tante Brigitte, with the promise to return to her for a couple more days before the end of my vacation and the return back to my place in the United States. At this point I felt almost like an expert at packing a suitcase, but that is what one must do when visiting several family members at different destinations.

The next morning found me on the bus headed south, and since I was already just minutes away from the border into Austria, we left Germany in no time. The next border crossing was several hours later into Switzerland. My seat was in the second row behind the driver, which gave me an almost unobstructed view of the wonderful landscape and made me feel like my head was on a swivel. Finally, we reached the foot hills of the Alps, but in no time the mountains were getting more impressive and outright regal in their appearance. The road took us over the Brenner Pass and through a couple tunnels. At one point the narrow one lane wound around a mountain at a forty five degree angle to the left where you had no view of what was coming at you. It seems the rule was whoever came to that spot first had to blow their horn and then proceed around that tricky turn. As we approached, we heard a car horn and had to back up a bit to let the vehicle with the right of way pass. By now the lady seated behind the driver was really freaking out, so I offered to change seats with her. While backing up, it appeared as if the entire rear end of the bus was hanging over the edge of the road with a drop into a deep canyon. In reality the rear tires of the tour bus were barely making contact with the ground, which gave me some concern about the driver's ability. But I dare say he must have done this maneuver several times and knew his stuff. The most dangerous part must have been behind us, I hoped, and started to enjoy the beautiful scenery. We traveled through the Dolomites, which have a beauty all their own and very different than the mountain peaks. At last, we reached the first town in Italy named Verona that everyone knows from Romeo and Juliette fame. We saw the special balcony that was a little disappointing. I thought it would be bigger and more elaborate, but instead it looked down right ordinary and crummy, not at all like in the movies. Oh well, the next stop was Venice, an all-time favorite city for years to come. I still long to make a journey there sometime before I get too old to enjoy any travel. As I should have expected, the once charming, but old wooden house which we occupied so many years ago was no longer there. The grounds were exactly the same, a new and more modern two-story house stood in its place, and the surrounding looked a little like a city yet to be. The young and friendly couple who occupied the house came out to greet my brothers and me. They knew from one of their parents that a refugee family had occupied the place so many years ago. They offered to take us on a little tour of the surrounding area, which we appreciated very much. The little Cape Cod house was gone without even as much of a hint that it ever existed, also the well had disappeared without a trace. I remembered schlepping water with my Brother all winter long. The small and the big farm houses were gone as if they never existed either. I was very glad the three huge oak trees, that saved our lives, still remained. We had reserved a few rooms in the nearby town and spent the night, after a hearty evening meal with the young couple as a thank you for giving us the tour earlier. Unfortunately, the young man wanted to talk only about politics that made my brother and me a little uncomfortable, after that evening, we were never in touch with them again. But I chose to remember that whole evening as a nice time spend. Soon we were on our way north again, but not without failing brakes and a delay over much needed repairs to the car. I laid out the money for that unexpected mishap, which mother reimbursed after our return. This surprised me immensely. For the duration of that trip my sister-in-law and I were relegated to sit in the backseat of the car, once in a while I would have loved to switch seats with the brother in the passenger seat up front, but no way, the guys pulled rank simply for being males. Oh poo, sexist pigs. By now I had enough of the both of them. I was looking forward to being home again, I mean back in N.Y. Before my flight I spent a few wonderful days and evenings with my new friends in Hamburg that I was staying with on this trip. Over the ensuing years I would visit and stay with Heike and her husband Kalle at least once every year. I was not able to stay with brother and sis-in-law, because they did not have a guest room in their charming apartment, plus the fact that both were absolute chain smokers and I had to step out onto the balcony every thirty minutes or less just to get a breath of fresh air.

It is high time I bring all this to a close. I was very concerned about my dear Brothers health. He lost a lot of weight and his skin looked sallow and shockingly unhealthy. My dear brother died of lung cancer, this was not very shocking for me, and I could actually see the end coming in his face a couple months before it happened. I am glad that I was with him as he passed on. The moment he was diagnosed, my sis-in-law quit smoking cold turkey, you see, it can be done if you really want to, and no excuses. She did a great job de-stinking her apartment not only with paint, but also some new furniture and carpeting. It is a pleasure now to visit with her.

On the home front, I had an unfortunate medical incident. After stepping out of the shower one morning, I must have fainted without any warning. When I woke, I found myself naked on the bare tile floor and completely unable to get up. I spent two days and two nights on that bathroom floor, then two of my dear friends and neighbors, who had not seen me outside came to investigate. One of them had a key to my house, where they found me and immediately called 911, the medics rushed me to the hospital, where I was diagnosed with A-fib, and the doctor advised me not to live alone anymore. This news put a definite wrinkle into my life style, and I fully imagine the same is to say about my youngest daughter. She, her dear husband and my grandson, welcomed me with open arms, as it was decided I would move in with them. Their instant decision to move in with them was very moving to me, and action was taken immediately. I have a most charming room with the paint color of my choosing, a beautifully redone floor, and I do feel at home with my own furniture surrounding me. To sleep in my own bed was a wonderful happening. There is only one drawback. The overabundance of house pets, namely three dogs and four cats, is quite hard to take for me. I shall try and do my best to adjust, with the oldest dog peeing in the house, due to some medication she is on. It is also not unusual for one of the cats to have an accident on a somewhat regular basis. My room is a pet free zone, thank goodness. But I have to be real diligent about that, as they try to sneak in whenever I open a door. My daughter is a real gem and keeps track of my daily medication intake. My dear son-in-law and grandson accepted my moving in without hesitation and helped in making me comfortable. After living with my daughter for one year, I am missing being at my house in Wilmington, N.C. and would not mind driving there by myself, the guest room furniture is still there, no problem as to where to sleep, and someone could get comfy on the blow-up mattress. Most likely for just one or two nights. Well, I did make the drive to NC with my buddy Miss M., a friend of my daughters. No problem except for my car having one hick-up. I had my mechanic in Wilmington check everything out, and $300. Plus 5 hours later we were good to go. I just wish our attempt to return to GA had been as easy as the trip to Wilmington. I swear, nothing ever goes smooth with me, sure enough I got us lost. Thank goodness for nice truckers we met at a rest stop, one such gentleman lends me his GPS with our destination entered, it got me home with verbal instructions every step of the way. Yes, I did send his device back to him with many thanks and a check of appreciation made out in his name.

Well, it is now fifteen months later. It has been a royal pain in the neck and other places to deal with all the paper work that resulted from the move to another state. You'd think it would be simple to move from North Carolina to Georgia, but you would be wrong. The United States are not all that united, with every one of them having their own rules and regulations. There is a mountain of paper work involved. Address change with the post office is the first step in a long line of paper work, which my gem of a daughter took care of for me. She had to make endless telephone calls with much time on hold with several agencies. Then you need a new driver's license and plates for the car, as well as insurance and on and on. My wonderful daughter took care of quite a bit for me, most problematic were all the things pertaining to my health. She is an absolute champ, and I am very lucky to have her in my life. I am not the only challenge for her. Among the herd of pets is one aged dog with a breathing problem, she sounds like a ninety-nine-year-old man with emphysema. The heavy wheezing and coughing all day long and every day makes you believe today might be the very last day of her existence on this planet. But she just keeps on wheezing and coughing, while trying to shake off her diaper that is securely fastened to her, because of her daily accidents of urination, due to some pills she must take for her thyroid and congestive heart condition. These accidents wreak havoc on the hard wood floor. Not a pleasant thing to deal with for my daughter under any circumstances. I am so looking forward to a visit to my house in North Carolina, a completely pet free zone. I don't need, nor want all that drama. But at this point I am not allowed to drive my car, my tags have been rendered suspended, to my surprise, so I'm informed per letter from the Motor Vehicle department. Pui, I say to that. Now I must register my vehicle in Georgia, etc., before I'm mobile again. There is no way of escaping on a moment's notice. I am itching to be at my home in Wilmington, N.C. All in due time, I guess. With the weather approaching super-hot, I hope the pool at my daughter's house will be ready soon. Over the past months the wheezy dog had fallen several times onto the still covered pool. We are sure her vision is no longer good enough. The weather got much warmer, and the pool was as anticipated finally uncovered. Sure as shooting, old wheezy fell in at the deep end, but without hesitating she swam like a pro across to the shallow end. I was standing alongside the pool and was expected to jump in and pull out the dog, but I did not do so. By the time my son in law jumped in and lifted her out it was too late. I am of the firm belief she had a heart attack, for I do not believe anyone or anything can drown in under two minutes or less. My old back problem, a result of a sport injury at age 15, reared its ugly side in the form of lower back pain. After being on my feet just a short time I have to sit or lay down for a few minutes. This happens even while shopping at a store, then I have to find a place to sit. This is no problem while in a department store, I just look for a chair or a bed in the furniture section and take my rest. The problem in a grocery store has me look for a sturdy shelf or a stack of soda six packs I pile up to sit on. I do sometimes get stares from other shoppers, but I just smile and say I needed a rest.

In the meantime, I have been approached by at least two publishing companies, who want to publish my auto biographical outpourings for a specific sum. I would love to be a published author, let's just see what is next, plus how much this will cost me. Frankly, I feel I should be paid for putting my whole life on display. After a bit of back and forth I decided to go with one of the publishers, now it is high time I finish my writing. In the mean time I had several dates to have a necessary Ablation, which is to cure the A-fib condition. This procedure was cancelled several times, either the insurance would not pay any part of the operation. My insurance was for North Carolina, but my daughter lives in Georgia. The dear child had to make numerous phone calls to get that straightened out. Then the doctor called everything off, I gather he was sick, because the flu has been making the rounds. My next appointment is in 2 days of this writing, on Nov. 7th, and I hope there will be no more cancellation. I'm tired of waiting around, for I have plans to visit my Aunt, who lives in N.Y. I will stay with her for about a week, during which time she will want to play a couple German board games with me. While staying with her, I will try to go to the German butcher shop for some really great sandwich meats, not available in Georgia. Oh, my goodness, when I think about food, I get the urge to travel to Germany, where the food is just stupendous. In the meantime, I will just dream on.

Well, I had my Ablation and feel pretty good but also very lazy. At this point I am spending far too much time in bed just "relaxing." I have to change my daily routine or get fatter by the day from too much relaxing. Setting up a daily, or better yet, a weekly plan will straighten me out for sure. At least I hope so. My dear Daughter oversees my daily taking of the pills and does not yet trust me to be on my own. I have decided to sell my house in N.C., which is a five-hour drive from my daughter's house, way too far for any quick getaway. Therefore, I will be looking for a nice two-bedroom apartment in a community with a nice pool hopefully near my daughter. She would prefer a big enough house for all of us, but I prefer again to be in a no animal zone. If I had my way, I would prefer to move back to N.Y. I miss it very much. per doctor's appraisal, my living alone days are over, oh my gosh, I have at last reached the old fart stage of my existence.

The only excitement I can expect now will most likely come from publishing my memoirs. At this age of 81, the only news will mainly be a notification of the passing of a dear friend, as I experienced today. Today I was informed of the death of an old friend and name sake that shook me up, she did have a nasty cancer and the outcome was almost expected. But when it happens, it is still a great shock. Today is Dec. 3rd, 2018. At 1:39 am, already past time for bed. Good night all.

Well, I did make a trip from Georgia to my house in North Carolina, accompanied by good friend Maddie, another octogenarian, oh drat fiddles, we are both 81 and still a bit sassy, at least I am... The car hick upped once on the way there, but after a stop at a road side rest area, she started right up again. After reaching my house I got an appointment with my regular mechanic to give the vehicle a once over. $300. And 5 hours later all was okay again. See what I mean? This confirms that I am a bit foggy, because I have already mentioned this a little earlier. I did not nearly get to do all I wanted to, like packing some cold weather clothes and some Christmas decorations, since I will be at my daughters for the Holidays, but at least I went to my bank to reload my wallet. So, after only two days we were again on the road back to Georgia. I'm not exactly sure how I did it, but it did not take long for two 81-year-olds to get lost. With the help of a very nice truck driver at a rest stop and his charger plugged into my "smart phone" the devise talked us all the way home. I'm telling you, the world is full of wonderful people, who are willing to help out.

Now I'm back home again, however, my aunt Lotte wants me to visit very soon, but this time I will be flying to New York. It would be too long a drive there anyway. My next task is to look up cheap flights to NY. At least my health is okay enough to travel. Furthermore, I am paid up to have this mini book printed and published. I do have to smile at the thought that I might soon be a published writer. This just cracks me up, what next?

www.ingramcontent.com/pod-product-compliance
Lightning Source LLC
LaVergne TN
LVHW012045070526
838202LV00056B/5600